Somebody Knows, Somebody C

Somebody Knows, Somebody Cares

Reengaging Students through Relationship

Edited by

Kirsten Hutchison
Deakin University, Australia

and

Tricia McCann
La Trobe University, Australia

SENSE PUBLISHERS
ROTTERDAM/BOSTON/TAIPEI

A C.I.P. record for this book is available from the Library of Congress.

ISBN: 978-94-6300-131-1 (paperback)
ISBN: 978-94-6300-132-8 (hardback)
ISBN: 978-94-6300-133-5 (e-book)

Published by: Sense Publishers,
P.O. Box 21858,
3001 AW Rotterdam,
The Netherlands
https://www.sensepublishers.com/

Printed on acid-free paper

TABLE OF CONTENTS

1. When One of the Teachers Smiles at Me: The Advocacy
    Model in Schools   1
    Bernie Neville, Kirsten Hutchison and Tricia McCann

2. Backgrounding Advocacy: Research Informing
    Advocacy Models   13
    Bernie Neville

3. Principles and Outcomes of the Advocacy Project   25
    Tricia McCann and Brendan Schmidt

4. Volatile and Vulnerable: Engaging Adolescent Learners through
    Advocacy and Mentoring Program   37
    Kirsten Hutchison

5. 'I Want Them to Listen to Me'   55
    Tricia McCann

6. Running in Quicksand: Stories from the Field   69
    Caroline Walta and Kirsten Hutchison

7. You Can't Do Advocacy for 15 Minutes a Day: Whole School
    Approaches to Advocacy and Mentoring   83
    Kirsten Hutchison and Don Collins

8. Electronic Support for Advocacy   97
    Stacia Beazley

9. The Heart of Advocacy: Implications for Schooling   111
    Kirsten Hutchison and Bernie Neville

BERNIE NEVILLE, KIRSTEN HUTCHISON AND TRICIA MCCANN

1. WHEN ONE OF THE TEACHERS SMILES AT ME

The Advocacy Model in Schools

WHY ADVOCACY

Until fairly recently, research on school dropout or failure focused on the reasons why many students do not complete their schooling: e.g. young people drop out or fail because they are not motivated, are not committed, have no self-esteem, have no ambition or, have no skills. These factors were then conventionally related to factors outside the school: inadequate family support, poverty, peer pressure, minority status, demands of part-time jobs. More recently it has become apparent that it is as reasonable to talk about 'problem schools' or 'problem classrooms' as 'problem students'. Poor motivation, low aspirations, low self-esteem and generally negative attitudes may indeed be brought to the school, but they can just as well be produced by school experience. There are clearly a variety of dimensions of school experience which may produce the outcome of disengagement and dropout, but to focus on conventional factors such as school size, curriculum content, school structure and material resources, is to overlook overwhelming evidence that it is the inability of schools to meet the developmental needs of students which is crucial.

The problem of designing appropriate educational provision for young people belongs within a much larger context, in which many adolescents in both urban and rural communities are seen to be 'at risk'. The label of 'at risk students' is variously interpreted, but in the Australian context it is currently employed to include students whose development into happy and productive members of society is perceived to be problematic because of disability, homelessness, drug taking, exposure to sexual abuse, poverty, poor motivation and achievement in schooling, exposure to health risks, criminal activity, and lack of employment opportunity.

There is an assumption, or at least a hope, that the dangers for these young people and society at large would be minimized if the education system could provide a way of managing the later years of schooling, which could engage, motivate and support students, and give them the knowledge and skills to gain immediate employment or proceed to further study. There is plenty of evidence that young people who fail to complete twelve years of schooling are at greater risk of unemployment, mental illness, substance abuse and incarceration than those who finish their schooling.

There is a common view that 'at risk' students can be most practically identified in terms of literacy, numeracy and school attendance and retention. It appears that

K. Hutchison & T. McCann (Eds.), Somebody Knows, Somebody Cares, 1–12.

successful programs for 'at risk' students are those which keep students at school for an extra year or two, or assist them to move from school to a job. Various school-based and community-based 'dropout prevention' programs have been tried in Australia and elsewhere. They have achieved various levels of success. Analysis of successful programs strongly suggests that one of the most potent approaches is the provision of mentors or counsellors to help students deal with the issues which lead them to disengage from schooling (Brooker, 2011).

INTRODUCING ADVOCACY

During the nineteen nineties the State education system of Victoria was dragged, with considerable resistance, into overt acceptance of an economic rationalist ideology. With some significant exceptions, the senior management of secondary schools became accustomed to the notion that the only basis for valuing schooling is its contribution to the GDP. Curriculum came to be valued for its contribution to the employability of students, rarely for its contribution to the intellectual, interpersonal, moral, or aesthetic growth of either students or the wider community. Where once it was conventional, or at least not ridiculous, to talk of students as persons with potential to grow, and the school community as a rich environment for intellectual, emotional and social growth, it became conventional to adopt a rhetoric which describes students as customers, or even as products fashioned to meet the needs of employers.

During this decade the public education system in Victoria was subjected to a number of cost-cutting measures which led to a reduction in school staff. Usually the first ones to get notice were staff such as welfare coordinators, counsellors and guidance officers who could be let go without interfering with the school's core business. By the end of the decade these apparently non-essential services had all but disappeared in Victorian State schools. Not surprisingly, this had unfortunate consequences for students, especially those labelled 'at risk'. Truancy rates were up and more 15–18 year olds were dropping out of school – or any sort of education – as soon as they could.

To its credit, the conservative Kennett government acknowledged that there was a problem and attempted to do something about it. In 1998 Education Minister Philip Gude approved funding for a project aimed at a radical transformation of the way teachers related to senior students. The 'Advocacy Project' developed and tested a model in which each student would have a teacher who was committed to meeting with them regularly for a conversation about their learning and anything that helped or hindered it. The project started in a small way, with a three-school pilot project and a focus on improving the attendance and retention of post-compulsory students. The incoming Bracks Labor government continued the funding and support. Over the next four years, the project was so successful in achieving this objective that it expanded to over 150 Victorian state schools, in which a significant number of students were able to spend fifteen minutes each fortnight with a teacher-advocate who was committed to listening to them and helping them deal with whatever issues – academic, psychological or social – they were currently confronting. It became increasingly clear that students in primary and middle school, as well as senior school were helped emotionally and socially, as well as academically, through having a teacher-advocate. Students with advocates were more likely to come to school each day, more likely to stay at school and more likely to feel good about themselves. They were also likely to get better academic results (Ocean, 2001).

However, in Education as elsewhere, innovations have a brief shelf life. When it had become patently clear that the Advocacy model could deliver what it promised, other projects were prioritized and funding for Advocacy ceased. Apparently, once we know that that something works, we do not need to do it any longer. It's much better to find some strategy which has failed in the UK or North America and adopt it as a creative response to a uniquely Australian problem.

Nevertheless, a number of Victorian schools, inside and outside the State system, manage to find the resources to provide their students with mentors or advocates. They are driven by the same conviction as impels some schools to engage chaplains. Their experience tells them that we cannot expect children and adolescents to focus on their schooling unless their social and emotional needs are attended to. One way of doing this is to make sure they have a reliable and trustworthy adult to talk to. There is overwhelming evidence that children who have such a person in their lives are much more likely to complete their schooling and grow into happy and productive adults than those who do not. It is not always possible for parents to fill the role.

Between 2008 and 2012, a group of researchers from La Trobe University, several of whom are authors of chapters in this collection, conducted a research project, *Engaging adolescents in schooling: A longitudinal study of student use of electronic self-assessment tools within Advocacy models of student support*, funded by the Australian Research Council. The aims of the project were to examine the impact of an Advocacy model of student support on adolescent engagement in learning on students in regional/rural and low-socioeconomic metropolitan areas. The implementation of the Advocacy Program in schools included the use of an online set of learning tools, the Student Self-Assessment Inventory (SSAI), later renamed the Student Achievement Inventory (SAI), developed in collaboration with teachers and students, which were designed to compile and report on students' learning goals, attitudes, values, opportunities, challenges, school connectedness, emotional wellbeing and career plans. The intent of the researchers was to further refine a flexible model of Advocacy to fit the needs of a range of schools, which would be effective in engaging students in learning and potentially, radically change the culture of middle years and senior secondary education by reshaping teachers' roles and student attitudes to learning.

In the post-compulsory context in which the Advocacy model was tested and supported, its appeal to school principals came primarily from evidence that adoption of the program would produce measurable benefits in the form of higher university entrance scores, lower exit rates and a smoother transition from schooling to employment, and would enable them to demonstrate accountability within this framework. These outcomes of the program are certainly to be valued. However, these outcomes are not the only outcomes to be sought through student advocacy, and the sterile ideology that has driven Australian schooling in its' recent unfortunate history is not the only ideology that can justify a society's commitment to education and its' expenditure on schools.

THE AIMS OF EDUCATION

Whatever our politicians might think, teachers do not get up each morning filled with the desire to contribute to Australia's economy by fashioning skilled and compliant workers for industry. They have many different ways of explaining why they stay in such a difficult and under-valued profession, and we do not need to list them here. Rather, what we want to do is point briefly to a broader view of education. There are other aims of education and other arguments for introducing some form of student advocacy.

We might argue, for instance, that the primary function of schools is the education of aware and engaged citizens of a democratic society. If the message of schools is that the more powerful members of a society have the right to command the less powerful members, irrespective of whether the latter believe it is in their best interests, they will carry this message into their adult lives. Unless the students in our schools experience democratic processes in their schooling and come to take responsibility for the impact of their actions in the community to which they belong, they are unlikely to develop the attitudes and skills required of members of a mature democratic society. The Advocacy Program is designed to educate students in democracy. It is built on the notion that mature democratic societies and organizations are founded on mutual respect. It acknowledges the reality that contemporary Australian teachers actually have little coercive or positional power over students and that the attempt to exercise it is often counter-productive. In a democratic model of education, positive teacher-student relationships and productive learning environments are defined in terms of power distribution and recognition of student rights — freedom, privacy, choice, due process and participation in decision-making. In implementing the Advocacy Program, teachers and students engage in a collaborative exercise to pursue the best interests of the students. The experience of a reliable relationship with a teacher who is genuinely interested in their wellbeing, listens with respect to their concerns, understands them well enough to offer appropriate advice when it is asked for and is willing to hand them power over decisions which affect them, enables them to approach their schooling as a cooperative venture in which they can choose to be engaged without the need to preserve their adolescent identity through resistance.

We might follow William Glasser (1997) in arguing that we each distinguish between a 'quality world' (which comprises the core group of people who satisfy our needs for belonging, power, freedom and fun) from the rest of humanity (which is either irrelevant to our need-satisfaction or blocks such satisfaction). Glasser suggests that if a teacher and the subject she teaches belong within an adolescent's quality world, they will choose to engage with the subject and learn. If not, they will quite rationally choose not to learn. The Advocacy Program represents a systematic approach to satisfying the needs of 'at risk' students by providing a safe environment where teachers demonstrate that they care for students, where coercion is eliminated and where students are given the opportunity to choose.

We might follow Carl Rogers (1980) in arguing that the quality of relationships between teachers and students is critically important for students' learning. Good teacher-student relationships have a rather wider effect than simply making schools nicer places to be. We have strong research grounds for arguing that they make a critical difference to students' academic learning, self-image and social adjustment (Cornelius-White, 2007). Or we can point to the extensive theory and research within neuroscience and cognitive-behavioral psychology on the impact of an emotionally supportive environment on cognitive processing. Research on the interaction between the human emotional system and cognitive system has led to the conclusion that 'facilitative' or 'supportive' environments, which produce 'positive affect', are critically important for cognitive processing (Panksepp, 1998). One of the well-documented effects of good teacher-student relationships is the perception by students that school is a safe place to be. The Advocacy Program acknowledges the impact of the teacher's friendliness and support on students' learning and the survival of 'at risk' students and sets out to make the school a safe place to learn.

We could argue from the research on *belongingness* that students' need to belong has to be satisfied in the school environment if the school is to have a positive impact on their learning and development. In her review of the literature on belongingness, Karen Osterman points to the evidence that the need to belong is associated with differences in cognitive processes, emotional patterns, behavior, health, and well-being (Osterman, 2000). There is strong evidence that the development of a positive sense of self and positive social attitudes, the establishment of academic attitudes and motives and the experience of successful participation in school processes, as well as academic achievement, are all directly related to belongingness.

Many, hopefully most, students have relationships with teachers and other students that enable them to experience the school as a place where they comfortably belong. Unfortunately, many students have no such experience. One of the strengths of a successful Advocacy Program, is that such students will have one person in the school who will take on as a professional responsibility, the task of establishing a personal connection with them.

We might argue further that anti-social, aggressive and self-destructive behavior among children and adolescents has its source in stress, and that an important way in which schools can respond to this problem is to meet their real needs, among which are a safe environment, caring adults and appropriate opportunities for learning. We can point to research in this framework that demonstrates the importance of

5

developing support systems that provide young people with a sense of connectedness, safety and capacity for initiative through relationships with caring adults (Maeroff, 1998). There is strong research evidence that the willingness of students to work for academic goals and to support each other in doing so, depends on their perception that teachers care about them as persons and as students (Harter, 1996).

The Advocacy Program is an attempt to take some of the randomness out of satisfying students' needs for safety and affirmation. Many students are lucky in the quality of the relationships offered them by their teachers. Others are not. Incorporating advocacy into a school's processes and structures is designed to ensure that the students in most need of a consistently supportive relationship will get it, and that the teachers most capable of providing it are given the support (and, where necessary, the training) to do so.

TEACHERS, MENTORS AND ADVOCATES

Schools are still constrained by an ideology that gives priority to what information and skills exiting students take with them from school to work. What ought to get more attention in a world where 'change is the only constant' is how they create a world through processing their experience. Although Newton's clockwork universe has long ago been replaced by a universe characterized by chaos and complexity, no longer built of 'things' but of relationships, schools are still expected to treat knowledge as a 'thing' to be transmitted, possessed, measured and traded for a prosperous life. We should not be surprised to find many young people reluctant to accept this nonsense. They are, however, interested in experience and apt to be engaged by an education that takes experience seriously.

Many adolescents attend school reluctantly. It is a huge part of their lives but they find neither meaning nor purpose in it. The Advocacy Program introduces an invitation for regular reflection with a skilled and caring adult on the personal experience of learning and the meaning of this experience for one's life. The advocate's ability to assist the students in reflection and goal-setting, in developing awareness of the ways they learn best and the ways they resist learning, makes a significant contribution to the adolescent's identity-formation.

For a couple of decades, it has been unfashionable within State systems of Education to promote the notion that schools have any business focusing attention on students' psychological or spiritual wellbeing. Politicians of all persuasions have perceived the function of schools in terms of their contribution to the economy. However, it is becoming increasingly clear that this is not enough. Chaplains are welcome in many schools because school communities realize this. They are welcome because they are committed to attending to the social and psychological wellbeing of children, as well as their spiritual wellbeing – a task which teachers allegedly lack the time and skills to do. However, it is fair to ask whether it is necessary to bring in someone from outside to do something that teachers could be doing themselves.

The suggestion that teachers could be doing more than they are already doing is inclined to cause some palpitations in the profession. However, the reality is that in many schools teachers already do, as a matter of course, what some schools are employing chaplains to do. They don't limit their role to guiding (or pushing) their students through the curriculum. They have genuine relationships with them. They know which of their students needs special attention, which of them is having a hard time at home or at school, which of them is at risk in some way or other. They know how to listen to students, and how to talk to them. They take some responsibility for seeing that each student's experience of school is a positive one and that schooling is a meaningful experience for them. They are concerned about their students' psychological and social wellbeing, and are willing to engage with them as they construct the values and meanings which will shape their lives, though they are less likely than chaplains to label the needs thus addressed as 'spiritual'.

On the other hand, it must be acknowledged that there are plenty of teachers who strongly resist the notion that they should have a commitment to anything other than teaching their classes, or any responsibility for their students' social and psychological wellbeing. They are not trained for it and, anyway, they haven't time. They argue that welfare coordinators, school counsellors, even chaplains, are the people who should be bothering about this. If students need coaching in constructing a meaningful life, the school can initiate a mentoring system, which conventionally involves inviting people from outside the school community to act as guides for particular students.

Alternatively, schools can expand the role of teacher, encouraging teachers to take on a mentoring role with students, meeting with mentor groups of a dozen or so students each week, providing the students with the opportunity to use the group and the teacher/mentor to deal with whatever is important to them. Some commit to the Advocacy model as it was originally conceived, giving students a regular opportunity for a one-on-one conversation with a teacher-advocate about their learning. All of these approaches depend for their effectiveness on the quality of the relationship between adult and adolescent. They have all proved to be effective in dealing with students' needs and making school a meaningful experience for them.

Advocacy differs in some respects from mentoring as it is generally understood. The label 'advocate' has been adopted from the beginning, rather than 'advisor' or 'mentor', to emphasise a particular aspect of the relationship. The task of the teacher-advocate is not to manage the student's behaviour but to listen to the student and be a reliable support. This involves having an understanding of the student's background and motivation and being prepared to persevere with the relationship. An advocate is committed to making sure that the young person's point of view is heard if they are in conflict with a teacher or the school.

The role of teacher-advocate or school-based mentor is different from the conventional roles of teacher and counsellor. The focus is on the student's learning and what contributes to it or gets in the way. The advocate does not reprimand, evaluate, instruct, direct, interpret, control or even (most of the time) advise. Many of the teacher's habitual behaviours have to be abandoned in the advocacy role. It works best when the advocate is not the student's classroom teacher, because the classroom teacher's need to manage the student can get in the way of the student talking freely and the teacher genuinely listening. Besides, from the student's point of view it may be the classroom teacher who is the problem they need to talk about.

An Advocacy Program commits resources to encouraging teachers to do what good teachers have always understood to be necessary and have always tried to do. What is significant about it in the current context, is that it represents a re-valuing of the pastoral role of teachers, after a period in which it was unfashionable or unpolitic to give it any value at all.

I'M NOT A COUNSELLOR

The advocate is not the student's counsellor. She meets with the student to discuss learning, not social or emotional problems. The paradox in this is that the focus on learning provides students with the opportunity to deal with everything else. While students for the most part acknowledge that their conversations with their advocates are helpful with regard to their studies, they tend to be more appreciative of the chance to talk about things like friendship, family, hopes and fears. When they are asked what is good about having an advocate, they say that it is good to know that one of the teachers is interested in who they are and how they are coping with school (Ocean, 2000).

Not all teachers want to be advocates or mentors or have the skills to take on the role. Some of them see their role simply as teaching History or Mathematics and don't want to get distracted by caring about their students' psychological wellbeing and life outside the classroom. They act as though their students' engagement in learning is unrelated to their psychological wellbeing. Some teachers are unable to abandon the habit of judging, directing and reprimanding students – legitimate behaviours for teachers, but behaviours which are not compatible with an advocacy role.

Advocates need many skills which, hopefully, they share with counsellors. They must be able to listen. They must be prepared to understand the way each child or adolescent perceives their world. They must be prepared to stay the distance with damaged or 'difficult' students and not give up on them. They must be capable of understanding that a young person's behaviour, no matter how anti-social or self-destructive it may appear to be, is simply the attempt to deal with the world as they find it.

Teachers on the whole, do not choose their profession in order to focus on their students' welfare. Their focus is on their students' learning. One thing that sets advocacy programs apart from those which employ chaplains or mentors from outside the school is the principle that the teacher-advocate's central task is to support students' learning. This is where teachers' expertise lies, and this is the focus of their conversations with the children or adolescents for whom they take responsibility. This sits beside another principle which is equally important. Academic success, engagement in learning and psychological wellbeing cannot be separated. Advocates encourage students to talk about whatever is preventing them from making the most of being at school. Sometimes it is a welfare issue which needs to be referred to a different kind of expert. More usually, it is a learning issue which fits within the expertise of the teacher. Most often, all the student needs is to have someone listen and understand. Many students in our schools are at risk in one way or another, and having a reliable and trustworthy person to talk to makes all the difference to their lives.

WHY NOT?

Unfortunately, even when the long term benefits of an Advocacy program are glaringly obvious to school principals and their staffs, their enthusiasm is constrained by a lack of resources and the perceived need to chase short term goals. When they do take the plunge and commit substantial teacher resources to the advocacy approach to engaging students in schooling, they find that not only does it enhance the experience and satisfaction of the teachers who take on the role, but that it makes everybody's jobs easier. Often, students who have previously been labelled 'problems' begin to find that their experience of schooling need not be a bore and a waste.

We could justify committing resources to student advocacy on the basis of research into the effectiveness of specific 'protective mechanisms' which impact on the wellbeing and academic success of children broadly classified as 'at risk' (Pianta, 1999; Rutter, 1987; Brooker, 2011). This research suggests that positive adult-child relationships, even transitory ones, are a key protective factor in enabling at risk children to become competent students.

Teacher-advocates do not approach students to discuss welfare issues, but to help them reflect on how they are managing the business of being at school. As it turns out, once a trusting relationship has been established, students seize the opportunity to talk about welfare issues, but this is very much their own decision. They make this choice because they believe they have found someone who respects them, someone who is trustworthy, and someone who will not give up on them. The contact with a committed teacher-advocate not only makes their time at school more meaningful and satisfying, but makes a substantial impact on the kind of future they can expect.

There is persuasive evidence that the impact of successive adult-child relationships is cumulative, either for better or for worse: high-risk children's and adolescents' adjustment, self-image, success and retention at school are positively correlated with good teacher-student relationships and negatively correlated with poor ones (Gannezy, 1994; Werner & Smith, 1980). Research on adolescent resilience, focusing on successful students from high-risk environments, has provided strong evidence that positive, supportive relationships with peers, parents and other adults

9

are a major factor accounting for their staying at school and achieving academic success. The evidence suggests that encouraging teachers to develop friendship relationships with adolescent students, or simply increasing the time teachers spend with students out of class, provides protection against at-risk behavior and increases students' engagement in schooling (Brooker, 2011; Macmillan & Reed, 1994; Claudet, 1995).

In the following chapters, the authors explore some of these dimensions of advocacy research and practice, in a variety of contexts and from a range of academic and practice-based perspectives. In Chapter 2, *Backgrounding Advocacy,* Bernie Neville reviews the academic literature underpinning the notion of advocacy in education, relating to the proposition that students' wellbeing and learning is strongly influenced by the quality of their relationships with teachers. It focuses on important research and theory from the interconnected fields of teacher-student relationships, learner-centered education, learning environments, protective factors for at-risk students and the impact of emotion on learning.

In Chapter 3, *Building Blocks for Advocacy Work in School,* Tricia McCann and Brendan Schmidt describe the origins of an innovative foundational advocacy project, designed to support student learning and student engagement. The Advocacy Research Project particularly focussed on establishing advocacy relationships in schools, with professional development for teachers to become advocates. The evaluation found that when advocacy relationships were trusting and consistent, both teacher advocates and students reported deeper engagement with their schools.

In Chapter 4, *Volatile and Vulnerable: Engaging adolescent learners through advocacy and mentoring programs,* Kirsten Hutchison explores the intricacies of teacher and student relationships, drawing on a selection of teaching and learning biographies, developed through interviews with secondary students and their teacher/advocates over three years. She illustrates some of the complexities involved in adolescent disengagement with schooling and explores the impact of an advocacy model on the students' experiences of schooling, learner identities and aspirations. The teacher and student biographies demonstrate how relationships with teacher advocates or mentors are critical to engagement in learning for secondary students and lead to enhanced connectedness and commitment to learning, to the school community and to students' aspirations.

In Chapter 5, *I Want Them to Listen to Me,* Tricia McCann, reflects on her experience of implementing an Advocacy program in one school. She navigated the differing perceptions of the program held by teachers and students, together with the conflicting demands on advocates, as she undertook multiple roles as advocate, researcher and provider of Professional Development to teachers.

In Chapter 6, *Running in Quicksand: Stories from the field,* Caroline Walta and Kirsten Hutchison give voice to the challenges faced by students, teachers, and researchers working in secondary schools with high proportions of multiply disadvantaged students, located in economically depressed regional areas. The analysis focuses on a number of themes: the academic, social and cultural factors impacting on student performance in this setting; the variety of staff responses to management and support of students in need; the obstacles to the development of a co-ordinated whole school response to multiple forms of disadvantage and the impact of minimal support on those who attempt to advocate for students at risk. The chapter illustrates the complexities for educators working within contexts of multiple disadvantage. It underlines the need for school structures to support people in advocacy roles highlighting the positive impacts of advocacy where it can be meaningfully administered and sustained.

In Chapter 7, *Whole School Approaches to Advocacy & Mentoring,* Kirsten Hutchison, a university based researcher and Don Collins, a secondary school principal, engage in a dialogue about the power of advocacy and mentoring programs in defining and shaping school cultures. Their conversation foregrounds the importance of whole-school approaches to advocacy and mentoring programs, outlines key organisational features and highlights the potentially transformative effects on students, staff and school culture.

In Chapter 8, *Using Digital Data to Support Student Engagement,* Stacia Beazley documents the role of electronic questionnaires in assisting advocates and mentors in their work with students. The development of the Student Achievement Inventory (SAI), a set of online tools for students to create a profile of their interests, skills and attitudes, learning styles, goals and future plans, was a collaborative project between researchers from La Trobe University and a group of Victorian schools. The SAI enabled schools to compile critical information about how their students learn, their attitudes to various subjects and the ways they are taught, students' ambitions and the obstacles they face in making the most of their schooling. Use of the SAI by students encouraged reflection on their learning and scaffolded deeper understanding of their individual goals and aspirations for learning. This chapter describes the potential contribution this instrument offers to school information systems, advocates, mentors and students.

In the concluding chapter, *Implications of Advocacy Work for Schools and Teachers,* the authors, Kirsten Hutchison and Bernie Neville, outline the sets of knowledge and understandings about teaching and learning developed through the school-based advocacy programs described in this collection. Within a performative educational climate of outcomes driven performance assessment, the chapter reiterates the role of emotional and interpersonal relationships in good teaching and learning and argues for the acknowledgement, embedding and valuing of the suite of 'caring attributes' evident in advocacy and mentoring programs in professional educational settings.

REFERENCES

Brooker, M. (2011). *Youth mentoring as an intervention with disengaged young people: A literature review.* Perth, Western Australia: Report for the Department for Communities.

Claudet, J. (Ed.). (1995). *Waves of learning: At-risk students.* Austin,TX: Texas Assn for supervision and curriculum.

Cornelius-White, J. (2007). Learner-centered teacher-student relationships are effective: A meta-analysis. *Review of Educational Research, 77*(1), 1–31.

Garmezy, N. (1994). Reflections and commentary on risk, resilience and development. In R. J. Haggerty, L. R. Sherrod, N. Garmezy, & R. Rutter (Eds.), *Stress, risk and resilience in children and adolescents: Processes, mechanisms, and interventions* (pp. 1–19). New York, NY: Cambridge University Press.

Glasser, W. (1997). A new look at school failure and school success. *Phi Delta Kappan, 78*(6), 597–602.

Harter, S. (1996). Teacher and classmate influences on scholastic motivation, self-esteem and level of voice in adolescents. In J. Juvonen & K. Wentzel (Eds.), *Social motivation: Understanding children's school adjustment*. New York, NY: Cambridge University Press.

Knight, T. (1991). At risk schools: A problem for students. *Principal Matters, 24*, 15–17.

Maeroff, G. I. (1998, February). Altered destinies. *Phi Delta Kappan, 79*(6).

McMillan, J. H., & Reed, D. F. (1994). At-risk students and resiliency: Factors contributing to academic success. *The Clearing House, 67*(3), 137–140.

Ocean, J. (2000). *Advocacy training manual* (Unpublished). Melbourne, Australia.

Osterman, K. (2000). Students' need for belonging in the school community. *Review of Educational Research, 70*(3), 323–367.

Panksepp, J. (1998). The quest for long-term health and happiness: To play or not to play, that is the question. *Psychological Inquiry, 9*(1), 56–66.

Pianta, R. C. (1999). *Enhancing relationships between children and teachers*. Washington, DC: American Psychological Association.

Rogers, C. (1980). *A way of being*. Boston, MA: Houghton Mifflin Company.

Rutter, M. (1987). Psychosocial resilience and protective mechanisms. *American Journal of Psychopsychiatry, 57*, 316–331.

Wentzel, K. (1995). Social and academic motivation in middle school: Concurrent and long-term relations to academic effort. *Journal of Early Adolescence, 16*, 390–406.

Werner, E., & Smith, R. (1980). *Vulnerable but invincible*. New York, NY: Wiley.

Bernie Neville
Adjunct Professor
Faculty of Education
La Trobe University
Co-Ordinator, Bachelor of Holistic Counselling
Phoenix Institute of Australia

Kirsten Hutchison
Faculty of Arts and Education
Deakin University

Patricia McCann
Faculty of Education
La Trobe University

BERNIE NEVILLE

2. BACKGROUNDING ADVOCACY

Research Informing Advocacy Models

The advocacy project emerged from a particular understanding of the process of learning and teaching. It is an understanding which, unfortunately, has never been seriously supported by the politicians and bureaucrats who control the delivery of what they like to call the "provision" of education. Nevertheless, it is central to the way that many teachers understand their task.

For some teachers, the proposition that students' well-being and academic success is somehow related to the quality of their relationships with their teachers is too obviously true to require comment. For others such an assertion is a nonsense. Indeed, for the past couple of decades it has been unfashionable to make such a claim. Nevertheless, there is a good research basis for doing so.

The following review looks at four areas of research relating to the proposition that students' wellbeing and learning is strongly influenced by the quality of the relationships which they have with their teachers and that, if they do not have a relationship with a caring and trustworthy adult in their out-of-school life the availability of such a relationship in their school experience is crucial.

We have very credible theory and strong research evidence to justify the claim that the re-structuring of schooling to include a relationship-based element such as advocacy would be an effective way of dealing with the disengagement of the many students who attend school reluctantly, leave as soon as they can, and gain little from the experience. Too often, these students move into lives characterised by unemployment, depression and other forms of mental illness, drug dependence and anti-social or criminal behaviour. Underlying our understanding of the sources of this disengagement is the possibility, indeed probability, that in many cases it is not a fault in the student, but rather a fault in what their schooling offers them.

The original advocacy program was established and received funding as a "learning management" system, whose purpose was to halt the decline in engagement and retention in post-compulsory classes in Victorian public schools. However, it was based on the understanding that student psychological wellbeing and engagement in schooling are intimately connected and that initiating and developing respectful advocacy relationships between teachers and students might have an impact on the culture of a school. Specifically, it was proposed that if the advocacy model was applied as it was designed to do, the school culture would become more student-

K. Hutchison & T. McCann (Eds.), Somebody Knows, Somebody Cares, 13–24.

centred, more respectful of students' needs and perspectives and more supportive of students' emotional development, including their need to experience autonomy and relationship.

The following review focuses on relevant research and theory from these interconnected fields:

- The teacher-student relationship
- Learner-centred education
- The learning environment
- Protective factors for at-risk students
- Learning and emotion

A study of the research findings in these areas finds little difference between the patterns prevailing at the different levels of schooling. Accordingly, this review includes studies dealing with all levels of schooling, on the assumption that what is true at one level of schooling is generally true at the others. Likewise, it is assumed that what is significant for students in USA, Canada, Ireland and UK is likely to be significant also for students in Australia. Currently, there is no persuasive evidence to suggest otherwise.

While there is a wide-spread assumption that teacher-student relationships are important in schooling, not much attention is paid to the evidence that good teacher-student relationships have a rather wider effect than simply making schools nicer places to be. We have strong grounds for arguing that they make a critical difference to students' academic learning, self-image and social adjustment.

RESEARCH ON THE RELATIONSHIP BETWEEN THE QUALITY OF TEACHER-STUDENT INTERACTION AND STUDENT SELF-CONCEPT, MOTIVATION AND ACADEMIC ACHIEVEMENT

The major body of this research has its origin in the theory and research of Carl Rogers and his associates in investigating the impact of the counsellor-client relationship on the outcomes of counselling. Rogers himself proposed that the counsellor qualities which are critical in effective counselling are the same as the qualities which are critical in effective teaching. Between 1960 and 1980, there was substantial research undertaken within this framework on the impact of specific teacher attitudes and behaviours (empathy, acceptance, warmth, genuineness) on students' self-concept, learning and behaviour. There is abundant research evidence that the teacher's communication of these qualities is associated with positive learning outcomes for students at both primary (Aspy, 1977; Christensen, 1960; Flanders, 1967; Skinner & Belmont, 1993) and secondary levels (Boak & Conklin, 1975; Kratchovil, Carkhuff, & Berenson, 1968) and also for adults (Wagner & Mitchell, 1969; Neville, 1978). There is evidence likewise, that the level of teacher functioning (as defined by these qualities) has a positive impact on students' motivation and engagement in their schooling (Aspy & Roebuck, 1977; Moje, 1996), on self-concept (Aspy,

Aspy, & Roebuck, 1984) and on classroom behaviour (Stoffer, 1970). Research carried out by Carkhuff and his associates (1971) focused in particular on the impact of adult "helping" relationships on the behaviour and achievement of children and adolescents whom we now classify as "at risk".

Cornelius-White's (2007) meta-analysis of studies of the impact of positive teacher-student relationships (as defined within Rogers' person-centred framework) clearly demonstrates a positive association between the relationship variables and participation, critical thinking, satisfaction, math achievement, drop-out prevention, self-esteem, verbal achievement, positive motivation, social connection, grades, reduction in disruptive behaviour, attendance, and perceived achievement. Cornelius White's conclusions are supported by research conducted within other frameworks. (APA, 1997; Lambert & McCombs, 1998).

RESEARCH ON LEARNER CENTRED EDUCATION

Rogers' educational theory emerged from his experience and reflection on the process of what he originally called "non-directive counselling" and later renamed "client-centred therapy". By the time he published his reflections on education in his book *Freedom to Learn*, he was referring to "student-centred" teaching, placing it within the broader philosophical framework of "the person-centred approach". At the heart of this approach is not a set of techniques, but an attitude of respect for the subjectivity and autonomy of the individual, who is perceived to have within him or herself, the resources to make appropriate choices regarding what and how he or she learns. The constraints on this awareness and exercise of choice – such as fear, habit, negative self-concept or the desire to please – are minimised in the context of a non-judgmental relationship with a trusted person who understands, respects and cares about the client or student. Rogers' conviction that the provision of such a relationship enabled the student to choose and act in his or her true best interests was based on his notion of an "actualizing tendency":

> The person-centred approach depends on the actualizing tendency present in every living organism – the tendency to grow, to develop, to realise its full potential. This way of being trusts the constructive directional flow of the human being toward a more complex and complete development. It is this directional flow that we aim to release. (Rogers, 1986, p. 37)

The teacher or advocate may be confronted by an angry or depressed adolescent whose "actualising tendency" is difficult to detect behind the screen of self-destructive or anti-social behaviour. Nevertheless, if we follow Rogers in this "way of being" we will understand that student-centred teaching and advocacy is by no means a totally permissive, laissez faire approach which encourages young people to follow whatever impulse dominates their feelings at the moment. Rather, it is an approach which, while fully acknowledging a student's feelings and understanding that he or she has good reasons for feeling that way, encourages them to reflect on

15

whether this is what they really want. Central to Rogers' theories of therapy and education is the notion of congruence or genuineness. If the teacher/advocate can be genuinely himself or herself in the relationship, without being dominated by the expectations of role or status, the student can learn to behave likewise.

Within such a framework it is desirable that a teacher/advocate is not the student's classroom teacher so that the teacher roles of control and instruction will not inhibit the advocate's basic task of non-judgmental listening. The student's current life may be happy or miserable, the experience of school may be engaging or alienating, but somebody knows, somebody cares. It is the listening that makes the difference.

Since the publication by the American Psychological Association of Learner-centred psychological principles: *A framework for school redesign and reform* in 1997 there has been a great deal of attention given to learner-centred schooling, with little or no reference to Roger's theoretical contribution.,

Where research in this field originally focused on the tools and the individual learner, there has been an increasing focus on the need for these elements to be supported by an appropriate school culture, in which the teachers applying learning-centred principles are actually committed to the philosophical position in which the latter are grounded (Carr-Chelman & Savoy, 2004). The learner-centred model, when allied to electronic delivery, is most effective in a school culture which supports a flexible pace, respects individual needs, caters to different learning styles, allows diversity in assessment, support, and personalised attention (Murphy & Rodriguez-Manzanares, 2009).

When the Advocacy Project was set up in Victorian public schools in 1999 it was described as a 'learning management system", a description which by-passed the other envisioned consequences of its' introduction. This was in the context of an assumption that electronic delivery would increasingly become the norm, particularly in the senior school. The design of the one-on-one advocacy model was predicated in part on the need to meet the challenge alluded to by Murphy and Rodriguez-Manzanares:

> The ability of high school students to self regulate may not be well developed, particularly if they are coming from a classroom environment where that ability was not required. Promoting learner centredness in a context of distance learning may therefore require that teachers help learners to manage their autonomy and to self-regulate. (Ibid, p. 605)

Moreover, the advocacy model was grounded in the notion that the support and encouragement of autonomy and self-direction is desirable at all levels of schooling, in all content areas and through all modes of content delivery. Clearly many teachers are unwilling to accept this notion or, if they accept it in theory, are unwilling to change their behaviour to relinquish the control with which they identify in their teacher role. Lambert and McComb (1998), Wiemar (2002) and William (1996) draw attention to this phenomenon at various levels of schooling. It was proposed that the introduction of a one-on-one learner-centred, 'learning management system', at the core of which was a genuine and trusting teacher-student relationship, would have an impact on the culture of the school and extend to influencing teachers to adopt a more learner-centred approach in their classrooms.

RESEARCH ON MEETING STUDENTS' NEEDS THROUGH LEARNING ENVIRONMENTS

Theories of students' needs and rights lead to diverse and contrary recommendations: for more autocratic schooling (at risk students need order and direction); for more academically focussed schooling (at risk students need clear academic goals and strong academic support); for more vocationally oriented schooling (students need to prepare for employment); for more caring schooling (students at risk need emotional support). Most such recommendations are ideologically based, and can generally produce research findings to support them. Nevertheless, in the context of the present discussion, we can argue that there is a substantial body of evidence that the satisfaction of particular interpersonal needs is a significant factor in school performance and retention.

Glasser (1990, 1997) has introduced the notion of the "quality school", arguing that we each distinguish between a "quality world" which comprises the core group of people who satisfy our needs for belonging, power, freedom and fun, from the rest of humanity – which is either irrelevant to our need-satisfaction or blocks such satisfaction. He suggests that if a teacher and the subject she teaches belong within an adolescent's "quality world," he will choose to engage with the subject and learn. If not, he will quite rationally choose not to learn. Glasser documents the impact of a systematic approach to satisfying the needs of at risk students which includes the provision of environment in which teachers demonstrate that they care for students, in which coercion is eliminated and where students are given the opportunity to choose.

Elkind (1986) has argued that anti-social, aggressive and self-destructive behaviour among children and adolescents has its source in stress, and that an important way in which schools can respond to this problem is to meet students' real needs, for a safe environment, caring adults and appropriate opportunities for learning. Other work in this framework demonstrates the importance of developing support systems which provide young people with a sense of connectedness, safety and capacity for initiative (Maeroff, 1998) and with relationships with caring adults (Haynes, 1998). Likewise, there is strong research evidence that the willingness of students to work for academic goals and to support each other in doing so, depends on their perception that teachers care about them as persons and students (Wentzel, 1995; Harter, 1996).

Research-based discussions of the influence of the "caring school" on students' motivation and achievement are usually presented within a relational perspective, which sees caring as independent of liking, but rather as having the characteristics of acceptance, attention and valuing (Nodding, 1992; Thayer-Bacon, 1993), attitudes which teachers extend beyond the school to the students' families. Parallel discussions of the impact of the "democratic school" underline the importance of maintaining teacher-student relationships that are grounded in mutual respect and the teacher's willingness to hand students power over decisions which affect them. In this model, the good teacher-student relationship and the good learning environment are defined in terms of power distribution and the recognition of student rights – freedom, privacy, choice, due process and participation in decision-making (Pearls, 1991; Pearls & Knight, 1999; Thayer-Bacon & Bacon, 1998).

Until fairly recently research on school dropout focused on the reasons why individual students do not complete their schooling: e.g. young people drop out because they are not motivated, are not committed, have no self-esteem, have no ambition, have no skills. These factors were then conventionally related to factors outside the school: inadequate family support, poverty, peer pressure, minority status, or the demands of part-time jobs. More recently it has become apparent that it is as reasonable to talk about "problem schools" or "problem classrooms" as "problem students" (Eccles & Midley, 1989; Knight, 1991). Poor motivation, low aspirations, low self-esteem and generally negative attitudes may indeed be brought to the school, but they can just as well be produced by school experience (Wehlage & Rutter, 1986). There are clearly a variety of dimensions of school experience which may produce the outcome of low retention rates, but to focus on conventional factors such as school size, curriculum content, school structure and material resources, is to overlook overwhelming evidence that it is the inability of schools to meet the developmental needs of adolescents which is crucial.

RESEARCH ON STUDENTS AT RISK: PROTECTIVE MECHANISMS

Rutter (1987) and Pianta (1999) have summarised research on the effectiveness of specific "protective mechanisms" which impact on the academic success of children classified as at risk. This research leads to the conclusion that positive adult-child relationships, even transitory ones, are a key protective factor in enabling at risk children to become competent students. (Werner & Smith, 1980; Garmezy, 1994). There is persuasive evidence that the impact of successive adult-child relationships is cumulative, either for better or for worse. Research within Pianta's closeness/ conflict/over dependency framework indicates that high-risk children's and adolescents' adjustment, success and retention at school is positively correlated with teacher-student closeness and negatively correlated with teacher-student conflict (Pianta & Walsh, 1996; Baker, 1999). This supports Carkhuff's finding (1969) that "helping" relationships may be for either better, or for worse, and that it is the "level of functioning" of the teacher, counsellor or case-worker which determines whether the impact of the relationship is positive or negative. The relationship does not have to have any suggestion of "counselling". Further research on at risk students has brought renewed attention to the impact of caring student-teacher relationships and a relationship focus in schooling (Baker et al., 1997).

Research on adolescent resilience, focusing on successful students from high-risk environments, has provided strong evidence that positive, supportive relationships with peers, parents and other adults are a major factor accounting for their staying at school and achieving academic success (McMillan & Reed, 1994; Beck, 1997; Zimmerman, 1999). The evidence suggests that encouraging teachers to develop friendly relationships with adolescent students, or simply increasing the time teachers spend with students out of class, provides protection against at-risk behaviour and dropping out of school (Radwanski, 1987; Lawton et al., 1988; Claudet, 1995; Fashola & Slavin, 1998).

The decade prior to the establishment of the Advocacy Program saw the publication of a number of reports on the effect of consciously developing teacher-student relationships with high risk students within an advocacy, mentoring or monitoring framework. Such studies have reported a significant improvement in attendance, discipline, academic achievement and attitude to school in the targeted population (Abcug, 1991; Sanacore, 1991; Flippo et al., 1997; Evelo, 1996; Testerman, 1996). There are also available a number of personal accounts by teachers working with delinquent or behaviour-disordered youth, which emphasise the critical importance of establishing good relationships if this work is to be productive (Dolce, 1984; Howe, 1991). Another finding relevant to the advocacy model, is that high risk students are less likely to drop out of school if a teacher or teachers have managed to establish a positive relationship with the students' parents.

The research outlined above supports the recommendation reiterated by many studies of the management of at risk students: that a personal, individualised, connection with a sympathetic and skilful teacher is critical. There appears to be a strong case for arguing that in managing the learning of students whose engagement and achievement are problematic, schools should consider developing organisational structures which facilitate ongoing one-to-one attention, communication and monitoring of students by teachers who are both interested and skilful.

RESEARCH ON LEARNING AND EMOTION

Theories of teaching and learning used to ignore the role of emotions in the classroom, assuming that they were a kind of waste product which got in the way of the brain's more important functions, such as cognition, memory, decision-making and planning. It is no longer possible to make this assumption. Researchers such as Damasio (2003), Panksepp (2004), Ledoux (2003), and Davidson (2012) have produced ample evidence that in normal human functioning, cognition and emotion cannot be separated. Emotion and cognition work together to enable us to deal with and explore our world.

Thanks to new technologies including electroencephalography (EEG), positron emission tomography (PET), computerized axial tomography (CAT) and functional magnetic resonance imaging (FMIR) we know a good deal today about how our brains construct emotions. The new fields of interpersonal neurobiology (Siegal, 2007; Badenoch, 2008) and affective neuroscience (Panksepp, 2004; Davidson, 2012) are challenging many of our conventional understandings, particularly the notion that thinking and feeling are separate operations and that it is the teacher's primary task to engage students in the former.

It seems that our commonsense notion that we have a thought and it makes us sad does not sum up the process very well at all. On the contrary, it appears that in many cases what Damasio calls an "emotionally competent stimulus" (p. 55) in the brain's environment, automatically triggers activity in certain parts of the brain, most notably the amygdala, which is located deep in the temporal lobe. We become aware of this as a feeling, and this feeling generates thought. What the research shows us is that our bodies register emotions before we are aware of the feelings that accompany them. Indeed, the body-states which we feel as sadness, actually slow down our capacity to think. This would be of minor interest to teachers, were it not for the fact that a lot of learning theory assumes that learning is essentially an outcome of thinking, and ignores the role of emotion and feeling. The notion that feelings generate thoughts, rather than the other way round, obviously has implications for the way teachers approach their task. However, what is most relevant to the current discussion, is the evidence that a student's emotional state can enhance or inhibit their ability to learn.

To quote Damasio (2003), "the fluency of ideation is reduced in sadness and increased in happiness" (p. 101). Given (2002) points to the research evidence that learning can likewise be shut down by fear and anxiety, whether they are aroused by immediate events or have their source in childhood trauma, regardless of whether the fear or anxiety is present in awareness. She points out that "chronic disruptive behaviour may be symptoms of chronic stress syndrome resulting from ongoing responses to subtle fears" (p. 24). Similarly, Teicher (2006) observes that any animal exposed to stress and neglect early in life develops a brain that is wired to experience fear, anxiety, and stress, and suggests that the same is true of people.

If the infant's first experience is to resonate with the stressed and anxious inner worlds of her caregivers, or if she suffers neglect or abuse in her first months, the implicit memory of these experiences will be stored in her lower brain and constantly reactivated as she goes through life. She comes to school damaged, with a deep but dysfunctional knowledge of the world of relationships. Research is showing that negative experiences, especially in early life, damage our brains. Martin Teicher and colleagues (Teicher, 2002; Teicher, Tomoda, & Andersen, 2006) found that verbally abusive parents can cause lasting damage to pathways that regulate emotions and process language in their children's brains. We have known for a long time that exposure to physical abuse and neglect causes brain damage in children. In the past decade it has become clear that that simply witnessing violence has these consequences, as do verbal, emotional and sexual abuse. Some children and adolescents come to our classes damaged. Bullying and punitive teachers reinforce the damage.

The challenge for teachers is firstly to notice, secondly to care and thirdly to respond with empathy and integrity. The care system, which – like the fear system – evolved in us to enable the species to survive, is a command system that prompts us to particular behaviours to protect the young. The other side of this coin is the child's need for a trustworthy and reliable adult with whom they will feel safe, and peers to whom they can become emotionally connected (Cortina & Liotti, 2010). Along with this is a sometimes ambivalent yearning for attachment (Bowlby, 1982; Ogden et al., 2006; Knox, 2003) and a capacity to rewire her brain differently, if the opportunity is provided (Doidge, 2007; Schwarz & Begley, 2002; Panksepp, 2004).

New experiences structure the brain for the better. Our students' brains are sculpted by their experience. Research on brain plasticity is indicating that every positive experience, including the experience of positive relationships, grows new neural pathways in our brains, whatever our age.

For many, we hope for most students, remediation of damaging experience is not required. However, there are young people for whom remediation through positive relationships is exactly what is required. The brain of a damaged child who is held safely in caring relationships will change over time, even against a child's initial resistance. What is demanded of teachers and other involved adults is the tolerance to cope with the consequences of previous damage: non-judgmental empathy and the determination not to give up on the child. Not every teacher has the emotional resources for this task but this need can be met by training (neuroplasticity even extends to the brains of teachers) and by providing each child with access to a responsible and caring teacher-advocate.

CONCLUSION

There are other relevant fields of theory and research which could be included in this review. There is an emerging literature on the changing role of the teacher in an age where the teacher is no longer the distributor of knowledge. Teachers may cling to an outdated conception of their role and its significance in the construction and transmission of knowledge, but technologies of information and communication are speedily diminishing this role. It appears increasingly obvious that teachers must accept an identity as guides to learning rather than providers of knowledge. It is in such a context that advocacy claims a place in schooling.

We can find an extensive literature in the fields of counselling and developmental psychology – whether in humanistic-existential, psychoanalytic or cognitive-behavioural frameworks – which supports the notion that young people need to have a relationship with a trustworthy and caring adult who has their best interests at heart. We cannot assume that such a relationship exists within every young person's experience, nor can we always assume that when children place their trust in an older person outside the family that the latter has their best interests at heart.

The Advocacy Project was initiated as a means of dealing with a perceived problem of school engagement and retention. Objective evaluation of the project has demonstrated that this aim was achieved. Moreover it has become increasingly clear over a decade's experience that providing students with a consistent and trustworthy advocate/mentor who is tasked to listen to them, not to manage them, has very positive outcomes for their psychological and social wellbeing, not to mention their academic achievement.

REFERENCES

APA Work Group. (1997). *Learner-centred psychological principles: A framework for school redesign and reform*. Washington, DC: American Psychological Association.

Aspy, D. (1978). A human technology for human resource development. *The Counseling Psychologist Fall, 7*, 58–65,

Aspy, D., & Roebuck, F. (1977). *Kids don't learn from teachers they don't like*. Amherst, MA: Human Resource Development Press.

Aspy, D., Aspy, C., & Roebuck, F. (1984). Tomorrow's resources are in today's classrooms. *Personnel and Guidance Journal, 7*, 455–459.

Badenoch, B. (2008). *Being a brain-wise therapist: A practical guide to interpersonal neuropsychology*. New York, NY: Norton.

Baker, J. (1999). Teacher-student interaction in urban at-risk classrooms: Differential behaviour, relationship quality and student satisfaction with school. *The Elementary School Journal, 100*, 57–75.

Baker, J., Terry, T., Bridger, R., & Winsor, A. (1997). Schools as caring communities: A relational approach to school reform. *School Psychology Review, 26*, 576–88.

Boak, R. T., & Conklin, R. C. (1975). The effect of teachers' level of interpersonal skills on junior high school students' achievement and anxiety. *American Educational Research Journal, 12*, 537–543.

Bonk, C. J., & Cunningham, D. (1998). Searching for learner-centred, constructivist, and sociocultural components of collaborative educational learning tools. In C. J. Bonk & K. S. King (Eds.), *Electronic collaborators: Learner-centred technologies for literacy, apprenticeship, and discourse* (pp. 25–50). Mahwah, NJ: Erlbaum.

Carkhuff, R. (1969). *Helping and human relations*. New York, NY: Holt, Rinehart & Winston.

Carkhuff, R. (1971). *The development of human resources: Education, psychology and social change*. New York, NY: Holt, Rinehart & Winston.

Carr-Chelman, A., & Savoy, M. (2004). User-design research. In D. H. Jonassen (Ed.), *Handbook of research on educational communications technology* (2nd ed., pp. 701–716). Mahwah, NJ: Lawrence Erlbaum.

Christle C. A., Jolivette K., & Nelson, C. M. (2007). School characteristics related to high school dropout rates. *Remedial and Special Education, 28*(6), 325–339.

Cornelius-White, J. (2007, March). Learner-centred teacher-student relationships are effective: A meta-analysis. *Review of Educational Research, 77*(1), 1–31.

Cristensen, C. M. (1960). Relationships between pupil achievement, pupil affect-need, teacher warmth and teacher permissiveness. *Journal of Educational Psychology, 51*, 169–174.

Damasio, A. (2003). *Looking for Spinoza: Joy, sorrow and the feeling brain*. New York, NY: Harvest.

Davidson, R. (2012). *The emotional life of your brain*. New York, NY: Hudson St Press.

Doidge, N. (2007). *The brain that changes itself: Stories of personal triumph from the frontiers of brain science*. New York, NY: Viking.

Eccles, J. S., & Midgley, C. (1989). Stage-environmental fit: Developmentally appropriate classrooms for young adolescents. In C. Ames & R. Ames (Eds.), *Research on motivation in education*. (Vol. 3, pp. 139–186). San Diego, CA: Academic Press.

Elkind, D. (1986). Stress and the middle grader. *School Counselor, 33*(3), 196–206.

Flanders, N. A. (1967). Teacher influence in the classroom. In E. Amidon & J. Hough (Eds.), (1997). *Interaction analysis: Theory, research and application* (pp. 103–116). Reading, MA: Addison – Wesley.

Garmezy, N. (1994). Reflections and commentary on risk, resilience and development. In R. J. Haggerty, L. R. Sherrod, N. Garmezy, & R. Rutter (Eds.), *Stress, risk and resilience in children and adolescents: Processes, mechanisms, and interventions* (pp. 1–19). New York, NY: Cambridge University Press.

Given, B. (2002). *Teaching to the brain's natural learning systems.* Alexandria, VA: Association for Supervision and Curriculum Development.

Glasser, W. (1990). The quality school. *Phi Delta Kappan, 71*(6), 424–35.

Glasser, W. (1997). A new look at school failure and school success. *Phi Delta Kappan, 78*(6), 597–602.

Harter, S. (1996). Teacher and classmate influences on scholastic motivation, self-esteem and level of voice in adolescents. In J. Juvonen & K. Wentzel (Eds.), *Social motivation: Understanding children's school adjustment.* New York, NY: Cambridge University Press.

Haynes, N. (1998). Changing schools for changing times: The Comer school development program. *Journal of Education for Students Placed at Risk, 3,* 1–102.

Knight, T. (1991). At risk schools: A problem for students. *Principal Matters, 2*(4), 15–17.

Knox, J. (2003). *Archetype, attachment, analysis: Jungian psychology and the emergent mind.* New York, NY: Brunner-Routledge.

Kratchovil, D., Carkhuff, R., & Berenson, B. (1968). Cumulative effects of parent and teacher – Offered levels of facilitative conditions upon indices of student physical, emotional and intellectual functioning. *Journal of Educational Research, 63,* 161–164.

Lambert, N. M., & McCombs, B. (Eds.). (1998). *How students learn: Reforming schools through learner-centred education.* Washington, DC: American Psychological Association.

Ledoux, J. (2003). *The synaptic self: How are brains become who we are.* New York, NY: Penguin.

Maeroff, G. (1998). *Altered destinies: Making life better for school children in need.* New York, NY: St Martin's Press.

McCombs, B. (2004). The learner-centred psychological principles: A framework for balancing academic achievement and social-emotional learning outcomes. In J. E. Zins (Ed.), *Building academic success on social and emotional learning: What does the research say?* (pp. 23–39). New York, NY: Teachers College Press.

McMillan, J. H., & Reed, D. F. (1994). At-risk students and resiliency: Factors contributing to academic success. *The Clearing House, 67*(3), 137–140.

Moje, E. (1996). I teach students, not subjects: Teacher-student relationships as contexts for secondary literacy. *Reading Research Quarterly, 31,* 172–195.

Murphy, E., & Rodriguez-Manzanares, M. A. (2009). Learner centredness in high school distance learning: Teachers' perspectives and research validated principles. *Australasian Journal of Educational Technology, 25*(5), 597–610.

Neville, B. W. (1978). Interpersonal functioning and learning in the small group. *Small Group Behaviour, 9*(3), 349–362.

Nodding, N. (1992). *The challenge to care in schools: An alternative approach to education.* New York, NY: Teachers College Press.

Panksepp, J. (2004). *Affective neuroscience: The foundations of human and animal emotions.* New York, NY: Oxford University Press.

Pearls, A. (1991). Systemic and institutional factors in Chicano school failure. In R. Valencia (Ed.), *Chicano school failure and success.* New York, NY: Falmer Press.

Pearls, A., & Knight, T. (1999). *The democratic classroom: Theory to inform practice.* Cresswell, NJ: Hampton Press.

Pianta, R. C. (1999). *Enhancing relationships between children and teachers.* Washington, DC: American Psychological Association.

Pianta, R. C., & Walsh, D. (1996). *High-risk children in the schools: Creating sustaining relationships.* New York, NY: Routledge.

Purkey, W. (1978). *Inviting school success.* Belmont, CA: Wadsworth.

Rogers, C. (1971). *Freedom to learn.* Boston, MA: Chas Merrill.

Rogers, C. R. (1987/1990). A client-centred/person-centred approach to therapy. In H. Kirschenbaum & V. Henderson (Eds.), *The Carl Rogers reader* (pp. 219–235). London, UK: Constable.

23

Rutter, M. (1987). Psychosocial resilience and protective mechanisms. *American Journal of Psychopsychiatry, 57*, 316–331.

Schwarz, J., & Begley, S. (2002). *The mind and the brain: Neuroplasticity and the power of mental force.* New York, NY: Harper Perennial.

Skinner, E. A., & Belmont, E. J. (1993). Motivation in the classroom: Reciprocal effects of teacher behaviour and student engagement across the school year. *Journal of Educational Psychology, 85*, 571–582.

Stoffer, D. L. (1970). Investigation of positive behavioral change as a function of genuineness, nonpossessive warmth, and empathic understanding. *The Journal of Educational Research, 63*(5), 225–228.

Teicher, M. (2002). The scars that won't heal: The neurobiology of child abuse. *Scientific American, 286*(3), 68–75.

Teicher, M., Andersen, S., Polcari, A., Anderson, C., Navalta, C., & Kim, D. (2003). The neurobiological consequences of early stress and childhood maltreatment. *Neuroscience and Behavioral Reviews, 27*(1–2), 33–44.

Teicher, M., Tomoda, A., & Andersen, S. (2006). Neurobiological consequences of early stress and childhood maltreatment: Are results from human and animal studies comparable? *Annals of the New York Academy of Science, 1071*, 313–323.

Thayer-Bacon, B. J. (1993). Caring and its relationship to critical thinking. *Educational Theory, 43*, 323–340.

Thayer-Bacon, B. J., & Bacon, C. S. (1998). *Philosophy applied to education: Nurturing a democratic community in the classroom.* Upper Saddle River, NJ: Merrill.

Vallerand, R. J., Fortier, M. S., & Guay, F. (1997). Self-determination and persistence in a real-life setting: Toward a motivational model of high school dropout. *Journal of Personality and Social Psychology, 72*(5), 1161–1176.

Wagner, E. D., & McCombs, B. (1995). Learner entered psychological principles in practice: Designs for distance education. *Educational Technology, 35*(2), 32–35.

Wagner, H., & Mitchell, K. (1969). *Relationship between perceived instructors' accurate empathy, warmth and genuineness and college achievement: Monograph.* University of Arkansas.

Wehlage, G., & Rutter, A. (1986). Dropping out: How much do schools contribute to the problem? *Teachers College Record, 87*, 374–392.

Wehlage, G., Rutter R. A., Smith, G. A., Lesko, N., & Fernandez, R. R. (1989). *Reducing the risk: Schools as communities of support.* Philadelphia, PA: Falmer.

Weimer, M. (2002). *Learner-centred teaching: Five key changes to practice.* San Francisco, CA: Jossey-Bass/Wiley.

Wentzel, K. (1995). Social and academic motivation in middle school: Concurrent and long-term relations to academic effort. *Journal of Early Adolescence, 16*, 390–406.

Werner, E., & Smith, R. (1980). *Vulnerable but invincible.* New York, NY: Wiley.

William, P. A. (1996). *Relationships between educational philosophies and attitudes toward learner-centred instruction.* Paper presented at the Georgia Educational Research Association, Atlanta, GA, September 20, 2014. (ERIC No. ED406377)

Zimmerman, M. A., Bingenheimer, J. B., & Notaro P. C. (2002). Natural mentors and adolescent resiliency: A study with urban youth. *American Journal of Community Psychology, 30*, 221–43.

Zins, J. E. (Ed.). (2004). *Building academic success on social and emotional learning: What does the research say?* (pp. 23–39). New York, NY: Teachers College Press.

Zuba, M. T. (1995). *Wish I could've told you: Portraits of teenagers almost dropping out.* DeKalb, IL: LEPS Press.

Bernie Neville
Adjunct Professor La Trobe University
Co-Ordinator, Bachelor of Holistic Counselling
Phoenix Institute of Australia

TRICIA MCCANN AND BRENDAN SCHMIDT

3. PRINCIPLES AND OUTCOMES OF THE ADVOCACY PROJECT

The Advocacy Research Project (described in Chapter 1) was designed to support student learning and student engagement. At certain social and economic times, when homelessness and unemployment are rife, student disengagement from schooling emerges as a major challenge for education and society. Some adolescents come to feel that there is no future for them and school has no relevance. To attempt reengagement requires a multi-pronged approach. The Advocacy Research Project focussed on intensive collaboration within each participating school to establish an advocacy relationship between teachers and students, developing goal setting skills and metacognition through the use of online Student Achievement Inventory (SAI) and providing professional development for teachers to become advocates. Together these elements addressed the various issues arising from 'students at risk' research, which had also been identified by participating schools.The findings of the research indicated that when the advocacy relationship was trustworthy and reliable, both teacher advocates and students considered an Advocacy program to be successful.

PROJECT BACKGROUND

Prior to the development of specific program elements, Schmidt undertook a review of a range of studies, particularly those focussing on teachers' and students' views on adolescent engagement in schooling. Key issues identified ranged across curriculum, relationship, aspiration, and academic achievement. Curriculum issues included the challenges of provision of a relevant, interesting and broad curriculum, through implementation of teaching styles which treated students as adults and teachers who held high expectations of senior students. Many of the adolescents consulted in the research stated that they did not have someone they defined as a 'trusted adult' in their life, with whom they could share dreams, concerns and day- to-day stories. This being the case, it became evident that such a role needed to be implemented into an advocacy program as the basis for growth and achievement. Therefore, adult role modelling of networking, gentle mentoring around career advice, future planning and schooling needed to be incorporated into the role of teacher advocate. Schmidt concluded that advocacy involved multiple strategies:

The advocacy model developed in this project, while drawing on elements of other programs involves advocacy processes, information technology,

K. Hutchison & T. McCann (Eds.), Somebody Knows, Somebody Cares, 25–35.

knowledge management, social information, goal setting, current as well as past teaching and learning models, organisational leadership and the holistic relationship between teacher and student. (Schmidt, 1998: 36)

From its' conceptual beginnings, the Advocacy Program was intended as a whole school approach, starting in the junior secondary years. However, due to funding constraints, it was piloted with senior secondary students, as these were perceived as demanding times, when students required one-to-one support. The program was later refocussed to specifically address the issues of the middle years of schooling.

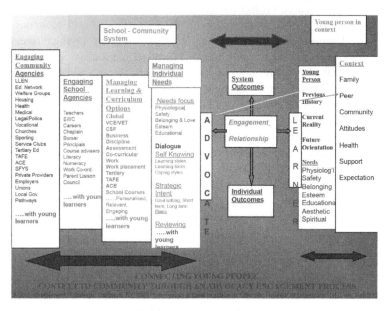

Figure 3.1. Contexts of student and advocate

Figure 3.1 above identifies various dimensions considered important in planning an Advocacy program. The heading of 'Young person in context' recognises the complexity of learners who emerge from their own individual context and their family culture. They have history, skills, beliefs, and attitudes that can profoundly influence their engagement with school. Traditionally schools attempt to acculturate the individual to the school's values and this may lead the student to feel disconnection or loss of feelings of belonging. The notion that the learner is central to the task of schooling has been subsumed by the many curriculum agendas imposed on schools and the various policies and procedures schools are required to implement. The advocacy project intended to return the student learner to the centre of the process of schooling and ensure that needs were met by a variety of specifically designed strategies.

When needs are not met students can disengage to the point of not reaching their potential, leaving school or suiciding and the end result can be tragic for individual, family and society. To ensure students remained connected to school became a priority of the project. How to successfully, economically and easily achieve this was problematic and continued to be explored. Theoretically, the schools and teachers involved in the project claimed to be student-centred, although this is challenging to define. A program evaluation described the advocacy relationship between staff and students:

> Advocacy is neither friendship, parenting, counselling, social work, nor teaching. It has elements of each and contradicts each in some respects. It is based on connection and trust, as friendship and parenting are: the skills needed include listening, attending and responding as counselling does; and it sometimes involves guidance by a more knowledgeable adult as teaching and social work do. (Ocean, 2000: 2)

The complexity of such a relationship is necessary to understand the Advocate dimension of Figure 3.1 above. 'Managing Individual Needs' requires skills on the part of the advocate to include personal and learning issues. To support adolescents' personal concerns requires attentive, empathic listening, without judgement or interruption. It also requires confidentiality within a relationship of trust, which may conflict with the need to mandatorily report situations involving homelessness or abuse.

In terms of learning issues, this listening may sometimes become problem solving, to address obstacles to learning, develop strategies or plan career and study pathways. It is important for the advocate and student to be aware of which kind of issue is being discussed and which approach is being used. For example, in the problem-solving approach, the advocate specifically directs the student towards particular action and behaviour. An alternate approach is to allow time for the issue to be resolved through dialogue and respectful listening, trusting that through the process of ongoing dialogue between advocate and student, a mutually acceptable 'solution' will emerge.

The 'Managing Learning and Curriculum Options' column in Figure 3.1 lists the varied options available to students who do not wish to attend University. Part of the advocate's role was to discuss with students their strengths, capacities, dreams and career aspirations. The advocacy project incorporated goal setting and questionnaires to support this aspect of the process. Many disengaged students lacked the required communication skills to negotiate with the school administration to present their points of view in any disagreement, which lead to numerous students dropping out and failing to pursue further study. A trusted adult who could represent the student in negotiations around discipline or general administration was pivotal in retaining students at school.

Schools and advocates encouraged the involvement of community agencies, such as sporting clubs, churches and employers, who provided external support for the families and peers of disengaged students to scaffold their pathways into employment.

ADVOCACY PROGRAM ELEMENTS

Advocate Role

The central element of the program was the appointment of a teacher/advocate to each student who would actively advocate on the student's behalf concerning learning, welfare and discipline. Apart from the important role of being a trusted advocate, the teacher would also be a 'knowledge navigator' (Schmidt, 1998: 36) who would:

> ...take full responsibility for the development of the educational program for that student and monitor the progress of that student, utilizing their professional role to the fullest. This is not the role for the teacher who wants just to give information to students. This [provides] proactive support for the whole individual, so that through the support the student stays at school and succeeds. (Schmidt, 1998: 36)

This aspect of the advocacy role focused on the aspects of learning that were problematic for the student and also those that were aspirational. The advocate supported the individual through skill and curriculum support. Since the Advocate was usually also a classroom teacher she was often able to adjust the student's curriculum or liaise with the student's teacher to meet the needs of the student. 'Students at risk' research supports this notion of one-to-one relationship and so the skills coaching aspect was important. Further, the formation of a relationship with a trusted adult, from whom students could seek advice on both wellbeing and academic issues was critical. One student stated, 'I go to the advocate for issues that are too small to take to the student welfare teacher, but too big to go away.' Professional Development for teachers was an integral element of the program and included administration and use of the online Advocacy tools, counselling skills in a student-centred process focused on listening and supporting students' welfare and learning issues.

GOAL SETTING

Teachers recognised that students found preparing or even thinking about their future difficult, as they had limited experience and knowledge of careers and study pathways. Students were unused to goal setting, planning action, implementing the plan, reflecting upon the outcome, learning from the process and setting a new goal. They did not understand problem-solving, how to break down the composite actions and plan for future behaviours. This process became an essential part of the advocacy relationship.

10 Goal Setting Plans were available on-line to students, accessible any time via an individual password. The plans varied from single goal-making plans, such as homework management, to those addressing life and career pathways. Because the goals were digitally stored, students had access to their plans for the duration of the advocacy project and built comprehensive records of their growth and dreams. This information initiated conversation between advocate and student, around commitment to learning, motivation and helped to establish trusting relationships.

Some of the Plans were designed to access information from the questionnaires in the Student Advocacy Instrument (See Chapter 9 for more details about the SAI), so that individual learning styles, learning skills and coping strategies could be integrated into their career plan. Advocate and student then used these plans to discuss educational pathways. It was considered essential that each student have regular sessions where goal setting was reviewed and monitored in a non-judgemental manner, so learning and career goals could be re-assessed and supported, as students' goals changed to incorporate new achievements in their academic and personal lives. Many students worked part-time outside school and developed skills they could incorporate into their learning programs and build on through their schooling experiences.

Web-based Questionnaires

Web-based questionnaires, located in the Student Advocacy Instrument (see Chapter 9 for more details about the SAI), were intended to provide students with information about personal learning styles, study strategies and approaches to learning. The questionnaires supplied targeted learning strategies that encouraged students to actively engage with learning and their future, as a personal quest,not simply in response to authority figures in their lives, such as parents and teachers. Teachers supported students to access on-line learning sites that could increase their curriculum options and support independent learning. The SAI allowed students to compile details of their paid and unpaid employment, work experience, interests and achievements, so they finished school with comprehensive records of their work histories for reference purposes.

Changing School Cultures

It was essential in the initial implementation phase that schools were committed to the project, since it is well known that when prospective reforms are not fully integrated into school organisation, they are at risk of failure due to lack of resourcing and support. Principals welcomed the possibility of positive change to school culture resulting from successful integration of the program components into the school. They were aware that supporting the work of advocates required time allowances, the development of new forms of individual support and the need for technical infrastructure to maintain a database of student learning profiles and track individual and cohort achievement and progress.

EVALUATION OF THE ADVOCACY PROJECT

The evaluation process gathered information about project implementation and student retention, supplemented by data regarding the perceptions of advocates, school leaders, students and other teaching staff. Evaluations of the three schools in the pilot program were undertaken on a three monthly basis throughout the first year of the Project and then on a yearly basis for the remaining two years of the pilot. The evaluation found that student achievement and participation were improved by the integration of the Advocacy Project into a school program. 'Students in the program passed, on average, 0.76% of an extra VCE subject in Year 11 and the exit rate was cut by one half to one third' (Ocean, 2000: 5). The retention rate was up to 250% better retention comparing advocacy and non-advocacy cohorts, attributed to the role of advocates in helping students with well-being and welfare concerns together with study concerns. The lower rate of absenteeism in the year 10 cohort was attributable to advocacy (Ocean, 2000: 14). The qualitative information indicated that the establishment of an individual relationship with an advocate whose role it is to support the student was an extremely powerful intervention.

The Advocate's Role

The evaluation found that because the advocate's role was multi-faceted, there were tensions in the requirements of the role. While recognising the existence of power imbalances between advocate and student in the school system, it was evident that since students were given opportunities to speak, be heard and supported, they had more power than the traditional teacher-student relationship allows. One of the teachers noted: 'I like the more equal relationship of advocacy' (Ocean, 2000: 32).

Advocates helped students with relationships, conflict with family, friends, teachers and concerns about schoolwork. Unless these issues were addressed as a priority, students could not concentrate on their schoolwork and almost all students had well-being issues at some time. Welfare issues, such as serious illness, poor housing, low income, drug and sexual abuse were initially discussed with advocates who subsequently referred students to School Welfare Coordinators, with access to relevant professional health, welfare and housing networks. Advocates provided an early recognition system for students at risk, who may not have accessed the Student Welfare coordinators of their own volition. Advocates also played an active role in supporting students in goal setting, devising learning plans, identifying learning styles, developing study skills and strengthening literacy and numeracy skills. As recounted in the evaluation:

Students live largely in a world of feelings rather than thoughts. This is why goal setting appeals to them. It is a way for them to move from decision based on feeling to decision based on thinking, which is more characteristic of adults. (Ocean, 2000: 7)

Advocates' Reflections

60% of advocates considered that participation in the advocacy project raised their job satisfaction as it allowed more time for individual students (Ocean, 2000: 23). Some teachers expressed fear of this aspect before beginning the project:

I find one-to-one flat, dull. (ibid: 26)

However, at the conclusion of the evaluation, 87% percent said they wanted to be advocates again the following year (ibid: 24), despite time pressures which often required advocates to use teaching preparation time to meet with students. The relational elements of the program were highlighted in interview data, which referred to processes of connection:

You build up a relationship and then they trust what you say. It's been a gradual development of respect for each other, a good friendship. I didn't go out of my way to get the kids to succeed. Whatever we focussed on was what the kids wanted. (Ocean, 2000: 28)

The student-centred aspect of the role was perceived as different and more challenging for some teacher/advocates than their classroom role. Advocates were encouraged to respect students as valuable people:

If I cancelled, I told them, because they would wait if I didn't turn up. Especially at the beginning of the year they would just sit and wait. I didn't want to waste their time. (ibid)

She needs someone to talk to who will listen. Kids feel really good if they've got an adult on their side. A lot of teachers yell and scream and don't listen. Kids need someone who will help them; who will go into bat for them. (ibid: 29)

Sharing experiences was considered an important aspect of the advocacy role. Some advocates shared parts of their own lives and ensured they made connections when students identified issues such as parental illness or death:

If there was any connection I could make, I did. (ibid: 24)

It is the connection with the kids that is important, not the formality of it. You don't need a formal structure. You need to connect with the kids. (ibid: 34)

Some advocates also gained insight into themselves as people and as teachers:

Personally out of advocacy I learned a bit about myself, how I go about forming relationships with kids. I put it under the microscope a bit. Before, I did this sort of thing with the kids I liked, now I do it with the kids I'm given. You might have to get on with a kid you don't like. (ibid: 27)

One advocate also discovered that one of his roles with International students was to offer cultural experience and interpretation:

They've used me as a cultural interpreter.... We do a session once a week and it's often about how to interpret the rest of the world. (Ocean, 2000: 38)

The contribution of a more mature, experienced perspective on the world provides an extra dimension for students who may not have other trusted adults in their lives. This advocate recognised the essential relational and purposive needs of the students, to help them unpack the techniques required for academic success:

These kids know they have to work hard and do well, but they don't know how. The goal setting helps them. They tend to assume there is only one way to learn. (Ocean, 2000: 38)

Teachers were aware that establishing and maintaining relationships with students required advocates to be non-judgmental and take up a person- centred approach:

They're not going to tell you their deep dark secrets if you judge them. You say, 'Why do you reckon that would be?' instead of judging them, instead of saying, "Well if you'd done that differently…". (ibid: 30)

Student Voices

The evaluation data was based on interviews with 49 students (25 females and 24 males) and surveys from 335 students. Over 90% of students wanted help with personal support, goal setting, problems with teachers, confidence building and improving their marks and study skills. 80% required career advice, 65% needed help in solving problems with friends and family (Ocean, 2000: 13). These needs are reflected in the following comments from students, collated from interviews:

I like that I've got someone to go to. I think it's good you've got someone to talk to. (ibid: 39)

They appreciated the one-to-one relationship and the sense that someone was exclusively listening:

I would recommend it to other kids. There's a lot of students who want to quit. I think if they had an advocate they'd want to come to school. I look forward to letting him know what I've done, that I got a good mark. (ibid: 40)

Some of these examples link to the parental element of advocacy, in that it provides the student with a reliable person, who is interested in their achievements:

> What's motivating is to tell him of all the positive things. If other kids had an advocate they'd focus more on the positive things. (But instead) they focus on the negative things. (ibid: 40)

As recognised by the advocates, the goal setting aspect of the role was particularly useful to some students.

> They help us find what we really want. Sometimes we don't know what we really want. They help you find the right direction. Mum and Dad had trouble keeping me at school because I have no goals. The small stuff gives you something to aim for, if you don't know what you want to do. I still don't know what I want in the future, but now I'm thinking about it. (ibid: 40)

Over 95% of students said they wanted their advocate to display commitment to equality, equal power, tolerance, fairness and mutual disclosure, friendliness, smiling and generosity. Students value qualities such as the ability to listen, encourage and reflect in a non-judgmental atmosphere, where student confidentiality and privacy is respected. This is reflected in this range of students' comments on issues of equality, friendliness and attentive listen:

> We like the equality; you're on the same level as them...You can be more equal and he's equal back....When there is more equality you don't argue as much, you respond better. I realise that if you treat teachers well, they'll treat you reasonably. You see them more as humans, more like people than you did before. (Ocean, 2000: 44)

> My friend has a good advocate too. She talks to him all lunchtime. They talk a lot. Like you do with your friends. It's more equal. I think it's good you have someone to talk to. (Ocean, 2000: 45)

Students also appreciated advocates who listened attentively and consistently, not just when action was needed, and who took students' problems seriously, however the advocate saw the issue personally (Ocean, 2000: 14). Interestingly, the relational cues that students interpreted as approachability often centred on smiling:

> She's always smiling, she's friendly. She tries to understand each and every person. (ibid: 45)

> Outside class he smiles. He says hello with a smile. Some teachers say hello and don't smile. (ibid)

> I felt uncomfortable. She never smiled. It was intimidating. If they are not usually smiling I would not talk to them. If they don't smile they're not listening to you, or we've done something wrong. (ibid)

Teachers may underestimate the impact of these small, interpersonal displays, which students in this advocacy program valued so highly.

The students who did not like advocacy (27%) were generally those who did not meet their advocates as regularly as was recommended, either through their own choice or because their advocate was not consistently available. When advocates met infrequently (once a month or less), students found this unhelpful. Some students had good support at home and so believed they 'did not need advocacy' (Ocean, 2000: 16). Other students considered advocacy to be 'nannying, patronising or controlling and did not need it' (Ocean, 2000: 16) or felt that their advocate did not have the necessary interpersonal skills to suppo rt them.

The element of trust was important when advocate and student met. Without trust, the relationship did not establish soundly enough to move forward. As advocates were chosen from amongst the teachers, students already knew a lot about the teachers' attitudes to students, because they had either been taught by them, personally observed them or knew teachers by reputation.

CONCLUSIONS

The Advocacy Project was designed to address the issues of disengaged students, with the intention of increasing school success and retention, through emphasising the teacher-student relationship. Instead of implementing new curriculum, the project resourced students with one-to-one advocates, web based goal-setting plans, and a student centred approach that empowered students to actively participate in decision making about their learning and future. In this context, advocates responded to the changing needs of the students and devised learning programs in negotiation with students, in order to build pathways into future employment and life dreams.

The person-centred approach of the project was designed to ensure students developed trusting relationships with advocates who actively engaged with their learning, administrative disputes, wellbeing issues and life and learning skills. Such a relationship supported the students' voices, through listening to concerns and providing support for student action on whatever issues emerged. The advocate monitored student concerns and learning and encouraged and supported achievement, planning and positive action.

REFERENCES

Ocean, J. (2000). *Advocacy evaluation* (Unpublished). Melbourne, Australia: Ocean Consulting.

Osterman, K. (2000). Students' need for belonging in the school community. *Review of Educational Research, 70*(3), 323–367.

Schmidt, B. (1998). *Report for corio community college: Meeting the challenges of a 'Wicked' environment: Draft report* (Unpublished).

Tricia McCann
School of Education
La Trobe University

Brendan Schmidt
School of Education
La Trobe University

KIRSTEN HUTCHISON

4. VOLATILE AND VULNERABLE

Engaging Adolescent Learners through Advocacy
and Mentoring Program

VOLATILE, VULNERABLE AND VISIBLE: INTRODUCING THREE STUDENTS

Caitlin's Story Part 1

13 year old Caitlin[1] was considered by her teachers to be one of the most troubled and troubling students in Year 8. She wore her school uniform with a contemptuous and defiant air: skirt hitched high, socks low, tie askew, her hair, tied up as required, was multi-coloured and decorated with an array of clips and slides. Her eyes were dark with eyeliner and each time we met for our interviews, she had another facial piercing and multiple earrings. In our first exchange she made it clear in the first minute that she disliked her secondary school and had not enjoyed the numerous primary schools she attended because the students were 'mean' to her and the teachers were 'terrible'. She was the oldest of six children: two brothers and a sister who lived with their maternal grandmother, another brother and sister who lived with her mother. Caitlin primarily lived with her maternal grandfather and his partner, although also often stayed with her aunt. She visited her mother, who suffered from mental health issues, on alternate weekends but was not in contact with her father. She had a pet rat, a boyfriend at the school and loved to shock people. She complained about the frequent detentions she was forced to attend, because she didn't do her work. In her opinion, too many of her teachers 'yelled' and forced students to do 'boring' tasks, which she saw no purpose for. One of her most hated subjects was Maths and the teacher was the object of Caitlin's derision:

> She teaches pointless things. Who is going to use algebra in the future? Seriously, it's gay.

In a recent Maths class, Caitlin had scored 10% on an algebra test. She organised a petition in the class, which all her classmates signed, demanding that they not do algebra, "because it is pointless." Insightfully, she reflected that her teachers would describe her as 'rebellious'. The school's Welfare Coordinator, who knew Caitlin very well, was frustrated by her lack of engagement in schooling, given her obvious potential as an intelligent and perceptive young person.

K. Hutchison & T. McCann (Eds.), Somebody Knows, Somebody Cares, 37–54.

Sam's Story Part 1

Fifteen year old Sam lived with his mother and older sister. He enjoyed primary schooling, where he played a lot of sport, excelling at basketball and was academically able, although 'easily distracted' according to his teachers. His transition to secondary schooling proved to be troubled, with Years 7 to 9 characterised by conflicts between other students and teachers and frequent suspensions from school. With a history of school avoidance, he was often socially isolated and he managed a range of mental health and substance abuse issues. He moved to Corella College in Year 10 and was impressed by the modern, high-tech facilities and the accompanying high teacher expectations and high trust environment he was welcomed into:

> Compared to my other schools, here it's like the teachers respect you, they get to know you, you know the teachers well, so there is a kind of a family atmosphere. They care about you and they help you, not just with learning, other stuff as well.

He enjoyed visual arts, photography and design subjects and was also interested in the humanities, particularly philosophy and history. He found Maths difficult, and speculated that perhaps his frequent absences during junior secondary school had resulted in crucial gaps in his conceptual understanding. Nevertheless, his intermittent attendance continued at the new school and was accompanied by erratic study habits and persistent failure to submit work. His teachers perceived him as a bright student with enormous potential and offered him a range of individual academic support to compensate for his lack of confidence and health concerns. While he had a friendship group, Sam was extremely sensitive and socially vulnerable within the school setting, sometimes choosing to isolate himself because of conflicts with other students.

Surfing Story Part 1

Jay, Corey, Alex and Lee were students in Years 7 to 10 at Callistemon College. Every Friday, if they worked well during the week, showed up at most of their classes, did what they'd been asked to do, not got into fights or sworn at teachers or insulted peers, if they stayed on site for the duration of the school day from Monday to Thursday, they earned a seat on the Surf Bus. With two teachers, a selection of their peers and a Callistemon alumni or two, they drove down to the coast in search of a wave. These students as a rule had not participated in extended swimming programs and were not strong swimmers. They rarely if ever left the city, apart from these Fridays. Their parents and carers were not in a position to take holidays or to buy them surfboards and wet suits, or drive them to the beach or pay for surf lessons. Some were anxious about leaving their inner urban neighbourhoods and began aggressive exchanges with their friends as the minibus hurtled along the freeway. The rules on the bus were different from the classroom, mostly unspoken until they were transgressed: no waving hands or pouring drinks or throwing rubbish or spitting out of the bus windows, no loud swearing that the teachers could hear, no rude gestures or *mooning** anyone from the bus.[2]

When they arrived at the beach, some took a long time to find a wetsuit to fit, struggle into it and collect a board. They did their warm ups on the sand with Lindsay, a music teacher and then listened as Frank, a senior maths and visual communications teacher, pointed out the break they would surf and the best route for paddling out. Suraya and Zoe, the only two girls on the bus, despite urging and teasing from the others, typically refused to put on wet suits and instead wandered along the beach with their sketchbooks and cameras. They photographed the sand dunes, waves, clouds, rock formations. When they reached the point, they sat by the rock pools, feet dangling in the water if it was warm enough, and drew the plants and creatures swimming in the shallow water.

One by one, the boys made their way to the water's edge, grimacing with the shock of the cold water on their feet. Once far enough in, gingerly they jumped on their boards face down and began to paddle, arms and legs flailing until they found their own rhythms. When they reached the area just beyond where the waves were breaking, they sat, bobbing with the rise and fall of the swell. Some gracefully moved to their feet and caught waves, shouting triumphantly, paddling out again and again. Others struggled to stand up, toppling, sliding, black bodies disappearing into the white water as the waves broke and water submerged them. Frank, Lindsay and Andy, the ex-student now passionate about surfing, directed the boys to the best positions, shouted instructions about when to paddle, when to stand, gave directions on how to turn the boards, stay on the wave, when to paddle through the lip of the breaking waves and when to slide off the board and dive into the wall of water before it breaks. The experienced surfers caught their own waves, seemingly effortlessly and gracefully standing up, long rides into the shore, sometimes diving into the water as their boards flew through the air. Gradually, when everyone became too hungry or exhausted, or the swell dropped off or it was time to leave, one by one the surfers came in, peeled off their wet suits and dressed. They piled back on the bus and headed to a nearby fish and chip shop. After their late lunch, one by one, a few of the students' heads started to nod, tired bodies slumped, the bus quiet as the students fell asleep on the long drive home.

BACK STORY 1

Adolescent disengagement from school is a critical challenge for contemporary societies. Since 2000, numerous Australian State and Federal government reports have investigated the problems of adolescent disengagement from schooling, early school leaving and consequent unemployment and disengagement from society. The 2013 report of the Foundation for Young Australians, *How Young People are Faring,* highlights the fact that while the proportion of young people (aged 15–24 years) in full-time education or training has increased, over the past decade from 44% in 2003 to over 50% in 2013, the proportion not fully engaged in work or study, or not in any form of education, training or paid employment, has also increased during this time. The labour force participation rate for 15–24 year olds has been in steady decline since 2008, with the largest drop in participation experienced by young males between 2008 and 2013: a decrease of more than 4 percentage points. Approximately one in five young people are not fully engaged in work or study, while just under one in ten young people are disengaged entirely from education, employment and training. Further, more than one in three unemployed Australians are young people, and the problem of youth unemployment is growing. The rise in youth unemployment is particularly acute among teenagers (aged 15–19 years), with 16.3 per cent unemployed as of January 2014 compared to 13.3 per cent in January 2008 (pre-GFC).

A high proportion of these unemployed teenagers are early school leavers, who may have either 'dropped out' or been 'excluded' for behavioural reasons. The negative consequences of this may include long-term unemployment, social isolation, depression and anxiety, substance abuse and self-harming behaviours. The groups most likely to disengage from school are indigenous youth, young people with poor English skills and those from the lowest SES areas (deciles 1–3) (Labour Force Participation: Data Profile 2014). Research on student engagement identifies school cultures as a key factor in early school leaving. Three school climate characteristics associated with early exit from secondary school are:

1. …..a non-stimulating environment with no clear relation to the wider community or adult world;
2. lack of support and referral to appropriate agencies for young people who are experiencing problems in their personal and academic lives;
3. and negative teacher/student relationships which are propped up by rules and regulations which disallow young people from expressing themselves as adult and responsible members of the school community (*Innovation and Best Practice in Schools*: DETYA 2001).

Nevertheless, while young people continue to believe that education is of vital and growing importance to their future employability and career options, the Mission Australia Youth Survey 2014 found high levels of concern amongst young people about coping with stress, school and study problems, with 40.7% identifying school or study problems as their major personal concern. This emphasises the need to support students to manage the demands of schooling and build resilience to the inevitable challenges arising from active and extended participation in education.

Restructuring learning as personalised or student-centred has been found to mitigate against disengagement. International research into high performing schools in high poverty areas has identified a suite of common characteristics: challenging curriculum that is connected to students' lives and to their communities; learning characterised by authentic tasks requiring higher order critical and creative thinking and exploration; teaching differentiated for individual interests, abilities and learning styles, which emphasises the development of skills of collaboration and communication and simultaneously emphasises deep understanding and student agency to shape their own learning (Walsh & Black, 2009; Kannapel & Clements, 2005). A common thread in research into adolescent disengagement from schooling is the importance of establishing a positive learning experience for students in the middle and senior school. The centrality of a one-to-one relationship with a caring adult, in shaping students' attitudes to schooling, their learning progress and decisions to complete their education is supported by a number of meta analyses (Brookes et al., 1997; Lawson & Lawson, 2013; Martin & Dowson, 2009). Overviews of school reform programs, in the search for common characteristics associated with 'effective schooling,' multifariously defined, have pointed to one-to-one relationships between a student and an adult as an essential component of programs leading to positive outcomes (Roorda et al., 2011). They argue that the empowerment of students in interaction with teachers is empirically supported as one of the best ways to improve student outcomes, especially for vulnerable students, since positive involvement with teachers is associated with engagement, well-being and achievement.

In particular, two relational processes have been identified as critical in building the capacity for strong advocacy and mentoring relationships: authenticity and empathy (Spencer, 2006). Authenticity is defined as "…being real with each other; being able to express genuine feelings and/or not hide feelings" and empathy as adults trying to, "…understand who the protégé is and what she or he wants" (Spencer, 2006: 296). Advocates and mentors can help students to regulate emotional reactions towards their teachers and their studies, by working towards understanding how reactive responses impact negatively on working relationships with teachers and peers and impede their learning. Advocates listen actively to the students' concerns, ask questions, challenge their perceptions and offer alternative responses, within a trusting environment, with the intention of enabling students to understand the difficult, challenging and stressful situations they find themselves in and develop more effective learning behaviours. It is these conditions of trust, authenticity and empathy that are central to the impact of the school based mentoring and advocacy practices.

The chapter explores the intricacies of these relationships, drawing on a selection of teaching and learning biographies, developed through interviews with secondary students and their teacher/advocates or mentors over a period of three years. It outlines some of the complexities involved in adolescent disengagement with schooling and explores the impact of advocacy on the students' experiences of schooling, learner identities and aspirations. It demonstrates that relationships with teacher advocates or teacher mentors are critical aspects of engagement in learning for secondary students and lead to enhanced connectedness and commitment to learning, to the school community and to students' aspirations. It also illustrates the ways in which teachers' emotional labour is an important dimension of their work as student advocates which influences their professional commitment and satisfaction.

BACK STORY 2: RESEARCH CONTEXT

The research described in this chapter was conducted within the context of the Australian Research Council funded research project, *Engaging adolescents in schooling: A longitudinal study of student use of electronic self-assessment tools within Advocacy models of student support.* (See Chapter 1 for background and details of this research project.) Twelve students were selected by teachers across seven participating schools, with between two and four students approached in the first year of the research, to account for any natural attrition through student mobility. The representative sample of students selected were of diverse ages, ethnicities, family backgrounds, gender and academic achievement. Students were interviewed twice yearly for a period of three years. 'Learning biographies' were developed from the interviews, exploring the impact of advocacy and mentoring programs on learning, well-being, engagement in education and connection to schooling. Narratives were analysed thematically and aimed to develop generalisations about the experience, needs, attitudes and identity-formation of the students; to assess the impact of advocacy and mentoring on their school experience and to generate useful theory regarding the relationships between schooling, identity and learning. Student interview themes included conversations around:

- Identity: period of time at school, hobbies and talents out of school, family, friends, languages spoken
- Experience of schooling: primary and secondary schooling history, favourite teachers and subjects, successes and struggles as a learner
- Attitudes towards schooling: perceptions of school, subjects, learning strengths and weaknesses
- Mentoring: experiences of mentoring, effects, changes in learning and perceptions of schooling and self-efficacy
- Aspirations for the future: 1, 3 and 5 year speculations about study, vocational and personal goals.

The researchers visited the schools regularly during the life of the research project, and interviewed principals, key members of the school leadership team, year level co-ordinators, student welfare staff, teacher advocate/mentors and students. We also spent time 'hanging out' at the schools, observing classes, looking at samples of student activities, exploring school websites, talking informally with students and taking tours of the schools with student or principals acting as guides. Our experiences and impressions of culture and climate at each school were shaped by our own histories and current institutional locations as education researchers. While each school leadership team began the research collaboration with enthusiasm and expressed strong beliefs around the value of the learner centred approaches and positive relationships between teachers and students, it was evident in schools with high numbers of multiply disadvantaged students that to effect any enduring change, even with the assistance of university partners, was extremely challenging. The introduction of ideas emphasising more equitable teacher – student relationships requires resourcing, and commitment by staff to rethink 'the ways things are' in school. To act as an advocate for students requires teachers to expand their capacity to listen without judgement and careful scaffolding to develop the mutual respect that is the essence of trusting and supportive relationships. In the second part of the stories from interviews with this representative selection of case study students and their advocate/mentors, we present examples of the diverse contexts in which such positive teacher - learner relationships have developed and illustrate their impact on students' learner identities.

Mentoring and Advocacy: Multiple Forms

Each of the participating schools approached advocacy and mentoring in unique ways. The key components of the Advocacy and mentoring program presented to schools were the establishment of organisational structures to support one to one relationships between students and teacher-advocates who undertook specific responsibilities with student/s. In some schools, this proved to be impossible and group mentoring, even at a class or year level was beyond the capacity of some schools' resources. In these instances, some students sought their own informal champions. A number of schools offered ongoing professional learning for teacher advocates, training them in counselling and advocacy skills, in order to model and scaffold the development of mutual acknowledgement and respect in any disputes between students, other teachers or the school. Other teachers drew on their own interpersonal skills or discipline knowledge in counselling or psychology and were not provided with targeted training. Similarly, while some schools embedded the development of study skills and meta cognitive and reflective techniques into the curriculum, to enable students to take responsibility for their own learning and academic progress, others were less explicit. Regular conversations between mentor/advocates and students, whether formally time tabled or occurring organically, was essential to the maintenance of trusting and mutually satisfying teacher-student relationships.

Caitlin's Story Part 2

> She [music teacher,informal mentor and advocate] knows like what I am into and she like, she understands, I don't know she is just down with us.

Caitlin attended Linden College, a culturally diverse secondary school community, where more than 80% of students come from families where 36 different languages other than English are spoken, including Turkish, Lebanese and Iraqi. Located in a growth corridor, the expanding school complex was surrounded by new housing estates and shopping centres in an outer northern region of Melbourne. Approximately 65% of students received a government education subsidy for low income earners. Although the school did not have a formal mentoring program, the Student Welfare Coordinators acted as referral services to link students and their families who required academic or personal support to the appropriate resources within and beyond the school. Four case study students were selected for tracking and interviewing twice yearly over three years, as they progressed from Year 8 to Year 10. Here we reconnect with two of them: Caitlin, introduced in Story 1 and her friend Jordan.

When Caitlin, was first interviewed in Year 8, she had very little to say about her schooling that was positive. While she enjoyed music and dance, she hated maths "with a passion", despised French, which was "pointless", did virtually no homework, did not attend the regular detentions she was given and refused to read anything ensuing from school. Caitlin argued that her lack of engagement was not simply that she found subject content boring and teachers uninspiring, but was directly related to her relationship with the teachers. Most of the time, teachers sent her out of their classes because of her lack of co-operation and insolence. She spent many hours sitting outside the offices of year level co-ordinators or student welfare counsellors. Caitlin felt she lacked relationships with adults who would help her to engage productively with schooling or act on her behalf; she had no-one who "knew [her] and cared". Her relationships with other students were similarly volatile, except with Jordan. He shared her passion for music but was similarly disinterested in all other subjects which he found irrelevant, boring and pointless. He initially described himself as a good student, who was well-behaved and co-operative in class, but, like Caitlin, he attributed his growing feelings of disconnection during Years 8 and 9 to his relationships with teachers.

Throughout Year 9, Caitlin and Jordan remained largely disengaged from schooling. Both were uncommitted to schoolwork, did minimal homework and devoted their evenings to Facebook and PlayStation. Caitlin's behavioural problems in class continued, with, she said, no consequences. Her grades fell from the As and Bs she had received in Year 7, to Cs and Ds. She again identified problems with teachers, who generally made no sense to her and thus, she found no value in asking questions in class. Teachers found her non co-operative, disruptive, argumentative. She was often asked to leave class to see the Year Level Co-ordinator for what she considered "simply telling it like it is." She described the year as "tough", since she was in danger of failing French and at risk of repeating Year 9. However, during the year, Caitlin developed a productive relationship with her favourite music teacher, which fostered at least some sense of connectivity and desire to take her learning and school experiences more seriously. Jordan too perceived his teachers, in particular the music teachers he admired as musicians and as teachers, as having a critical impact on his motivation, the quality of his work and his engagement in the subject. Although he was unenthusiastic about school, his interest in music and his friends was enough incentive to go each day. Like Caitlin, while he did not have a formal advocate or mentor, he related well to the year coordinator and by the end of Year 9 he also related well with the music teachers:

They stand out, they inspire, they are interested in you and they make you want to put the extra effort in.

Jordan did not directly attribute his more focussed attitude to this relationship, but he continued to prioritise music and worked hard to develop his skills and played in the two school rock bands with Caitlin. He began to realise that Year 10 was significantly more serious and required dedicated study habits if he wanted to succeed in life. He decided he was not interested in university, and that he would take up a trade and pursue vocational education.

Caitlin developed a passion for music, and committed to practising her instrument every day, the electric guitar, and played and sang in performances with the school rock bands throughout the year. While she had no formal music classes (it was an elective not offered in second semester) she identified the music teacher as a mentor. Caitlin's confidence was expanded through this relationship, which included phone calls and texts about performances. She felt the teacher understood her, listened to her and engaged Caitlin and her friends in making music, through mutual respect and a shared commitment to music. In participating in the school rock bands, Caitlin felt free to learn, teach and create with her peers and teacher mentors. This musical collaboration created a space for her to move between school-ordained tasks and her own interests, accessing music, and engaging with friends for their own pleasure. This "passionate affinity space" (Gee & Hayes, 2011), allows everyone to create, mentor and teach others and also makes it possible for everyone to learn, to be mentored and taught. Similar to Glasser's notion of "quality worlds" shared by teachers and students, referred to in Chapter 1, 'school work' and 'fun' merged as students accessed the available technological and human resources within the school and used them for meaningful, satisfying purposes. This music teacher also acted as an advocate in Caitlin's situation with French, and enabled her to progress to year 10:

> She saved me from getting kept down. I spoke to her about it and she said, "Oh don't worry, I will talk to Mr. X", and then she fixed it, everything, it was good. Because she's a muso she like, she knows like, what I am into and she like, she understands, I don't know, she is just down with us, I don't know how to put it.

Caitlin continued to encounter serious personal challenges: complex and volatile family relationships, a fear of the dark requiring a continuous television presence in her bedroom which resulted in insufficient sleep, and a history of bullying and violence throughout her primary and secondary education as both victim and perpetrator. Nevertheless, her perspective on schooling had changed dramatically by the end of Year 10. Through the informal advocacy and mentoring she received from her music teacher, she effected a suite of powerful attitudinal shifts. She found a more positive friendship group, made goals and exciting plans for her future, through consulting with careers advisors and her mentor about pathways into further education in music. Both Caitlin and Jordan found motivation and commitment to being better students through their music teacher advocates, because they were able to see themselves as valued, trusted and capable members of a community that validated their passions and developed their talents and capacities as learners.

Sam's Story Part 2: Connected Learning

Sam's move to Corella College, with its' focus on technology, flexible vocationally oriented pathways, and individualised, differentiated learning, was intended to maintain his connection to learning. He had been deeply unhappy at his previous secondary school. Volatile relationships with other students and teachers lead to daily conflicts, skipping classes, suspensions, school refusal and ongoing struggles to keep up with the academic demands. He came to "hate" some teachers and became seriously debilitated by the constant stress, which resulted in intermittent attendance, further isolating him from the possibility of friendships and academic growth. By contrast, Sam's experience of Corella College was largely positive, primarily because he felt a sense of belonging there:

> What is unique about this school is that they mention words like 'respect' and that the teachers know you well and you know them, so there is a kind of a family atmosphere, and that the learning really is individualized.

This focus on mutual respect, on teachers and students knowing one another as individuals was a defining aspect of the school's educational charter and served as the basis for implementing differentiated learning.

The open plan design of the school, with flexible learning spaces, glass walls between teaching and learning spaces and staff offices and large windows overlooking open, lightly treed bush land, fostered this sense of freedom and accountability. According to the Principal:

> That level of transparency, physical, virtual and inter-personal, is important in understanding the place of mentoring: it's made the school what it is.

Advocacy and mentoring were key dimensions of the school culture and contributed to teachers' workloads, rather than be perceived as pastoral care. Group mentoring sessions were time tabled each week for 75 minutes, typically with 8 – 12 students and one teacher, who taught at least one core subject to the mentor group students. The mentoring curriculum covered various dimensions of Social Education, such as Life and Study Skills and Drug and Sex Education. This regular small group time also provided an opportunity for group problem solving and discussion of any current issues of interest or concern. The sessions were also used to informally monitor academic progress and well-being and address specific individual needs.

At the heart of advocacy and mentoring is an authentic relationship between students and mentors which requires skilful management, as Sam's mentor Brooke explains:

The key to the Mentor Program is the development of that relationship with the student. You develop a really strong relationship with that student as their advocate and their mentor. You are also the disciplinarian. It is a tricky path to follow sometimes as a teacher, to work out, ok, I am advocating for this student and now I have to let them realize that what is going on is not acceptable. So if they start doing things they shouldn't, like missing school, you know how to approach them a lot better than the general class or form group teacher or year coordinator who has this multitude of students that they're responsible for and don't know particularly well. We come up with a way of talking about an issue that's taking a student off track. It is tricky, but I think once you work out how to do it, once you know the kid, you know what you can do. I think too another difference is that here, every kid feels like they are heard. Someone knows your name, you get noticed. Your mentor will say, "Hey, maybe you are not working hard enough or maybe you should start doing some maths homework more regularly."

From Sam's perspective, the impact of mentoring and advocacy was profound. At his previous school, his unexplained absences and increasing disconnection from his peers and teachers produced feelings of hostility and anger that ultimately forced him to leave the school. Although he continued to struggle with peer relationships and with managing the academic demands of Year 10, he was supported by Brooke to develop insights into his emotional reactions and respond with more maturity.

I have been like, taking days off and, like school has been getting to me. My mentor has helped with that, we can work out deals and ways to make things better, make things work for us individually. Instead of me being like, "Oh I hate school," and not doing anything, it can be, "Oh I hate school, but I can make this better for me if I just do this and in the long run that makes it better for you [mentor teacher] as well."

Brooke's role as a mentor and advocate crucially involved scaffolding students' capacities to reflect on their own behaviors and identify more useful strategies enabling students to take responsibility for their learning. This involved honest appraisals and shared problem solving:

I have some fairly strong mentees and they will say "*I* can't, *I* am not doing it," and I say "Okay fair enough, cool, *you* are not doing it, thanks for being honest about it. Let's work out what *we* are going to do to get around this." You have a discussion, but it is not like an airy, fairy discussion. Because these students know me and I know them, I can identify things that are and are not working for them and say, "You *are* doing this." So *we* talk, *we* work out how they can do what's challenging, when they feel like they can't do something. Then they say, "Oh yeah *I* am doing that and *I can* do this."

This modelling was important for students such as Sam, with histories of negative schooling experiences, who needed to develop different ways of coping with stressful situations and managing strong emotions. In their role as advocates, mentor teachers supported mentees in their relationships with other teachers and peers, modelling and scaffolding the process of taking responsibility for any misdemeanours and repairing the situation. In Brooke's words:

> You are there to help support them, even when they know that you know that they shouldn't have done it. Sometimes I have to mediate between the student and the teacher and say, "Hey, what are you doing? That was out of line." I think the advocate is important here, because it makes the student feel like they are respected a little bit more. Rather than, "You swore at a teacher, you are going to get suspended, have a meeting with the principal, see you later." Then that poor teacher they swore at doesn't have anything to do with the process, and the student is suspended for a day and comes back into their class and nothing has been worked out, they just have to pretend like that didn't happen, until it happens again.

Through the advocacy program at Corella, with the support of his mentor Brooke, Sam began to take increased responsibility for his own learning and educational trajectory. With his Year 10 peers, he developed insights into his own counterproductive patterns of thinking and reacting, as a consequence of the conversations arising from the mentor group's social education curriculum content. Sam and his peers increased their capacity to sustain productive interpersonal relationships with teachers and fellow students and make considered decisions about their learning.

Knowing the whole person beyond their academic achievements was crucial to the work of mentor and advocate, as Brooke explains:

> School is not just about what you got on your Maths test, it is also about how you are feeling inside. It is also about: Have you got that job yet that you really wanted? How is your arm going after you fell off the bike?… just that personal level. You are not going to know about every single student in the school, but you know your little group of ten.

The advocacy and mentoring process at Corella College enabled students and teachers to voice their critiques in a safe environment and negotiate solutions and modes of relating that were mutually beneficial for teaching and learning. Advocates modelled empathetic modes of communication, respect for individuals and scaffolded students into mature adult behaviours, by insisting that they assume responsibility for their actions. For Sam, this process was critical in maintaining his confidence and connection to learning and in shaping his aspirations for the future. As a Year 11 student, with his mother he attended various University Open Days and was contemplating an Arts degree, majoring in politics and history.

Surfing Story Part 2: "Life Isn't All about Just Doing Schoolwork ...It's about Going Surfing..."

Callistemon Community College was established in the 1970s during a period of intense debates about the purposes of schooling. Formal structures of education were being challenged by progressive thinkers in education, such as Ivan Illich, in his critique of institutionalised education systems, *Deschooling Society* (1971). In response to the idea of de-institutionalising and democratising schooling, a group of Melbourne educators established a mini school campus with a small group of students. The key principles were a non-hierarchical structure, which involved students in deciding how teaching and learning might best happen. In particular, the idea that education occurred not just in the classroom, but also beyond schools and in communities, was a driving theory. The school culture evolved and adapted over the ensuring years, with the principles of student involvement, teacher – student negotiation of learning and strong student – teacher relationships enduring. Many students lived with challenging family circumstances, had histories of academic underachievement or struggled with authority, prior to enrolling at Callistemon. The students enjoyed small individualised classes and a wide range of arts, sports, health and well-being programs involving community agencies and the Friday Surfing Program.

The multi-dimensional Surfing Program at Callistemon Community College offered enduring social, emotional, physical and educational benefits to students, involved staff, alumni and to the school community as a whole. According to Frank, the instigator of the program:

> One of the reasons I run it is because I feel like it is offering a wider version of the curriculum. I think education should also include learning how to enjoy life; this is what I believe surfing is about. It enables you to really be exhilarated at certain moments in time. It brings community into the school; whoever is on the bus that day has a real sense of identity, of belonging to that group which means you respect each other and you have to get along with the rest of the group. For me it is really valuable for building trusting relationships with students. When I see them during the school day to day, we know we have got that very special bond of jumping off the rock there at Eagle Point and you know, getting cleaned up. ... The memory of that sort of gets lost, but at those moments we can get back there again, so I think it is important that it is put away for later.

Students too agree that the program enriches teachers and student relationships, since the practice of learning to surf is grounded in trust, mutual respect and risk taking. Adam, a recent graduate of the school reflects:

> I think for the school, it's really a good way to get everyone to work together and be social and happy and bond with each other, because you know it can

be a bit intense in the classroom here. I think working on those things away from school in a really fun environment helps students to get along better and especially with the teachers as well. If you are more comfortable with the teachers on a personal level, you are going to find it easier to learn from them I think at school.

Students who may be regularly in conflict with one another in the stressful classroom environment develop tolerance for each other through being together in the bus, on the beach, in the ocean, as this exchange reveals:

Alex: I think surfing with people you don't always hang out with at school makes classroom life a lot easier as well, just being more comfortable with certain people...

Steven: Yeh, even if you don't like someone and you are out in the water with them, as your buddy, they are looking after you, you're looking out for them. So you can't hate them anymore, if something happens to them.

Alex: You have to trust them, obviously you are still alive and so it is all good.

Steven: You do get a little bit more courage, because you are there together in a group.

Surfing together also sustains a collective strength, respect and trust between students and teachers that translates into increased co-operation in the classroom:

Frank: When you have the surfing students in class, they're less likely to be maniacs so to speak, because you have that other relationship.

Alex: There is respect within that relationship. If you know a teacher well enough, I reckon if you play up, you just sort of feel bad inside.

The unique teacher student relationship developed through surfing impacts on classroom culture and on participating students' learning. When teachers know something of students' courage and triumphs in the water, when students have to trust that their teachers will keep them safe in the ocean, when students respect and admire their teachers' surfing prowess, a unique kind of radical trust relationship is forged, containing the possibility of embracing risks in the classroom. As Frank commented:

For me teaching practice is all about the relationships, especially at this school where you have some people who have more trouble with being able to focus and be attentive in class. If you spend some time quality time so to speak, in this case surfing, I think you can build a bit more honesty into the relationship. There is resilience within that, so you give a bit more feedback. If it is going to be a critical comment that could be taken the wrong way, you know that at least that you have a relationship with that person, so if they get a bit upset by what you say, they are going to be able to deal with it, they are not going to hate you for it and probably vice versa as well.

Managing fear is an inescapable dimension of surfing and provided students with regular opportunities to move beyond their physical and psychological limitations. These Year 9 students recognised that confidence developed through surfing at times translated into the confidence to tackle something challenging in class:

Jay: Because, like a couple of times there have been like really big waves, then you get the confidence, like you have got to try and go for it, and then like you try it and sometimes you make it. Then like in class, if you've got like a really hard sum or something, then you like, have a go at it, not just like saying, no it is too hard.

Lee: You can be frightened when the waves are huge or when you get held underwater for ages or wipe out really badly. You do get scared and then somehow you get through it.

Corey: Yeh our confidence gets over the fear.

Andy: Surfing involves pushing yourself. Before you hop in, the waves don't look too big but when you get in, it's really rough. You get out there and when the waves are towering over you, you think, either I can go in and surf the small waves in the shallow water, or I can fight the fear and get out to where the good waves are. That's the challenge. You really want to take the best opportunity that presents itself, so even if it is like a ten minute paddle past all of the smaller waves, you have got to really work for it and move against the current. You get there and feel huge satisfaction that you've made it. Then you have to catch a big wave to get back in.

Surfing helps to shape the identities of these students who have typically experienced failure at school, to feel more confident about who they are and about their capabilities because they face fear in the ocean and feel 'exhilarated' by the expansion of their physical and mental capacities through surfing. Teachers too share this experience of being energised by surfing:

Lyndsay: When I come back from surfing, I feel great. We have a great time, we enjoy it. I'm reasonably good at it and still getting better, so you feel like you take that with you. Like you may be crap at a few other things, but you walk around with that little spring in your step, thinking, "That was all right."

Similar to the "passionate affinity group" which was created between Caitlin, Jordan and their teachers at Linden College through their shared love of playing rock music, the surfing program provided a context for the development of strong, mutually respectful relationships between students and their teachers. These shared experiences engendered feelings of goodwill and trust between teachers and students which permeated classroom interactions and according to both students and their teachers, created unique opportunities for deeper engagement in learning at school.

CONCLUSION

Across these stories, it's evident that advocates and mentors made significant positive contributions to students' school experiences. All students identified relationships with teachers and advocates/mentors as the most influential aspect of their engagement at school. There existed a healthy diversity in the organisation of advocacy and mentoring programs in the schools participating in this study. Some advocates were assigned to individual students, while in other settings students sought out particular teachers who inspired them, were understanding, or were available to listen to their concerns. In each case, students reported that having such a support person made a crucial difference to their school experience, by increasing their connectedness to learning and the school community and allowing an opportunity to discuss personal concerns which impacted on their education. Teacher advocates modelled and scaffolded students' capacities for reflection on their responses, interactions and behaviours and analysis of their individual learning practices.

For some students, the relationship with the advocate assisted them to feel a sense of empowerment in their learning, for others it give them a sense that they were important, and thus a confidence and sense of being supported that was crucial to their ongoing positive experience at school. For all students, participation in an advocacy and mentoring process, either as a core program or informally, fostered continued self-reflection and connection to school and to others. This in turn, led to the development of clearer academic and vocational goals, a desire and also a capacity to be more organised with school work, and a deeper commitment to the choices they were making.

Finally, teachers involved in mentoring and advocacy programs experienced a deep professional satisfaction through this dimension of their work. Skilled mentoring and advocating for students demands and develops a sophisticated tool kit for managing and enriching students' learning behaviours and interpersonal skills. The professional learning and personal investment required to fully participate in mentoring and advocacy work in schools is both challenging and gratifying. As Melissa, an early career teacher at Callistemon College reflects on the centrality of teacher – student relationships to engagement in learning and satisfaction for students and teachers alike:

> I had a very traditional idea of schooling when I graduated and so when I got here it was obvious very quickly that this school was different. There was this constant negotiation between everyone, teachers and students alike, and the idea of relationship, everything was core around the relationships you have with everyone around here. I walked in and thought, I love this, and I just wanted to stay a part of it and 5 years later I'm still here. I think it draws people in, that's fundamentally important.

The enduring power of relationship is at the heart of sustained engagement in learning not only for volatile and vulnerable students, but for all learners.

NOTES

[1] All names of students and schools in this chapter are pseudonyms.
[2] Mooning is the practice of displaying one's bare buttocks by removing clothing, e.g., by lowering the backside of one's trousers and underpants, usually bending over. *Wikipedia.*

REFERENCES

Australian Workforce and Productivity Agency. (2014). *Labour force participation: Youth at risk and lower skilled mature-age people: A data profile 2014.*

Brooker, M. (2011). *Youth mentoring as an intervention with disengaged young people: A literature review.* Report for the department for communities, Western Australia.

Brooks, M., Milne, C., Paterson, K., Johansson, K., & Hart, K. (1997). *Under-age school leaving: A report examining approaches to assisting young people at risk of leaving school before the legal school leaving age.* Hobart, Australia: National Clearinghouse for Youth Studies.

Centre for Applied Educational Research. (2002). *Middle Years Research and Development (MYRAD) project executive summary* (February-December, 2001). A report to the learning and teaching innovation division, department of education and training. Melbourne, Australia: The University of Melbourne.

Cornelius-White, J., & Brown, R. (2006). Politicizing school reform through the person-centred approach: Mandate and advocacy. In G. Proctor, M. Cooper, P. Sanders, & B. Malcolm (Eds.), *Politicizing the person-centred approach: An agenda for social change.* Ross-on-Wye: PCCS Books.

DETYA. (2001). *Innovation and best practice in schools.* Victoria Government.

Fildes, J., Robbins, A., Cave, L., Perrens, B., & Wearring, A. (2014). *Mission Australia's 2014 youth survey report,* Mission Australia.

Foundation for Young Australians. (2013). *How young people are faring.*

Gee, J. P., & Hayes, E. (2011). *Language and learning in the digital age* (1st ed.). Abingdon and New York, NY: Routledge.

Illich, I. (1971). *Deschooling society.* New York, NY: Harper and Row.

Kannapel, P. J., & Clements, S. K. (2005). *Inside the black box of high-performing high-poverty schools.* Lexington, Kentucky: Prichard Committee for Academic Excellence.

Lawson M. A., & Lawson H. A. (2013). New conceptual frameworks for student engagement research, policy and practice. *Review of Educational Research, 83*(3), 432–479.

Martin. A. J., & Dowson, M. (2009). Interpersonal relationships, motivation, engagement, and achievement: Yields for theory, current issues, and educational practice. *Review of Educational Research, 79*(1), 327–365.

Roorda, D. L., Koomen, H. M. Y., Spilt J. L., & Oort, F. J. (2011). The influence of affective teacher-student relationships on students' school engagement and achievement: A meta-analytic approach. *Review of Educational Research, 81*(4), 493–529.

Spencer, R. (2006). Understanding the mentoring process between adolescents and adults. *Youth and Society, 37*(3), 287–315.

Thapa, A., Cohen J., Guffey, S., & Higgins-D'Alessandro, A. (2013). A review of school climate research. *Review of Educational Research, 83*(3), 357–385.

Walsh, L., & Black, R. (2009). *Overcoming the barriers to engagement and equity for all students.* Paper presented at Australian Curriculum Studies Association 2009 Biennial Conference, Curriculum: A national conversation, Canberra, October 2–4, 2009.

K. HUTCHISON

Kirsten Hutchison
Faculty of Arts and Education
Deakin University

TRICIA MCCANN

5. 'I WANT THEM TO LISTEN TO ME'

This chapter considers an Advocate's experience of implementing the Advocacy program, and the different perceptions of the program by teachers and students and the conflicting demands on the Advocate. In order to explore the phenomenon of Advocacy and adolescent meaning making, I acted as an Advocate in a Melbourne Northern Metropolitan secondary school for a period of fourteen months. This gave me an opportunity to work directly with students who were 'at risk' or in need of support, to establish a trusting relationship with students and to reflect upon these relationships. In these interactions, I heard the students' stories and provided them with support and advocacy, undertaking multiple roles within the program, such as advocate, researcher and provider of Professional Development to teachers.

The Advocacy coordinator in the school, 'Georgia', assigned me five students, each of whom granted me written permission to work with them and gather data. In the Advocacy sessions, students were encouraged to bring any welfare, educational, administrative or relational issues they had, so that we could speak about them and, if they chose, I could advocate on their behalf with the school in order to negotiate their concerns. The students used the sessions in different ways and for different concerns and as an Advocate, I needed to have wide ranging skills and strategies to meet their needs. When a student asked me to coach her in equilateral equations I did indeed feel challenged.

MY DIFFERENT ROLES WITHIN ADVOCACY

I held a variety of roles, each informing the other and the view I present here is based on the data that I gathered as a member of the Advocacy Research Project Team at La Trobe University. Through my role as a member of the Project Management Committee, I was able to meet with various stakeholders and become aware of various expectations and competing agendas. In my role as presenter of Professional Development, I co-provided a full day program which described the philosophy of the Advocacy Program, summarised the research upon which it was based and introduced the Student Achievement Inventory (SAI) and Questionnaires (see Chapter 8 for details of the SAI and Questionnaires), so Principals and teachers could make an informed decision about whether they wanted to implement the program in their school. After schools had made a commitment, I also provided specific

K. Hutchison & T. McCann (Eds.), Somebody Knows, Somebody Cares, 55–68.

Professional Development in *Counselling,Communication Skills*, and *Talking with Students* to teachers and support staff involved in the Project.

I undertook a third role for one year, as Advocate for the Advocates, to address issues that arose for teachers during the implementation of the Program. I visited schools on a regular basis to support the Advocates with any school administrative issues, such as arranging meetings or time allowance, provision of further professional learning or computer issues with the SAI. I was chosen for this role because I had an overview of the project and specific skills of facilitation and had met with most of the senior staff in the schools implementing the project. This role allowed for a less formal and more regular interaction between staff and designers.

The fourth role was as researcher for my PhD, which the study in the school was providing data for. In the researcher role I embraced a phenomenological methodological approach to adolescent meaning making and epistemological change. The theoretical stance underpinning my research approach was student-centred listening (Rogers; to read more about this, see Chapter 2) and the constructivist-developmental approach of Robert Kegan (1998). My final role was as Advocate to five students and it is this role that is central to this chapter, which is also informed by my experiences gained through my other roles. Consistent with my vision and that of the Project Management Committee, I was committed to being student-centred, to being aware of student welfare issues, and to allowing the students to guide discussions about their future and their learning.

I needed to have well developed counselling and listening skills in order to support students with their issues or problems. I needed to be prepared to advocate on the students' behalf and provide their story, in any interaction with the school administration. I also had the SAI to support our interactions, so that students could learn more about themselves and their choices. There were diverse views amongst teachers of what an Advocate should be and in the following section I will present some of these varying perspectives that emerged through the professional development I conducted. It is not exhaustive but reveals that teachers' perceptions of the purposes and practices of schooling and of the role of an Advocate are complex and varied.

TEACHERS' PERCEPTIONS OF THE ADVOCACY ROLE

Teachers' perceptions of the purposes of Advocacy programs in schools primarily centred on the capacity to positively influence student attitudes and behaviours. These perceptions were influenced by teacher priorities around the purposes of schooling and this shaped their perceptions of the role of Advocacy. The statements below emerged during teachers' discussions and questions during the Professional Development sessions. Since these comments informed my role as Advocate and some were present in the school as I was supporting students, I saw them as a Greek chorus, constantly chanting in the background. I therefore represent these teacher voices as chorus in this section. Imagine me as a lone person on a large stage, surrounded by these many voices, all demanding a particular Advocacy role.

Chorus One: You need to be the person who listens to her. She just needs someone to listen to her, she needs to tell her stories to someone who won't judge her and then she will grow of her own volition. Advocate reflections: This statement represents the people who prioritise interpersonal relationship with trusted adults as essential for students to reach their potential and stay engaged with school. It is consistent with the student-centred relationship approach. It often clashes with curriculum and rule centred chorus.

Chorus Two: You need to be the expert in the relationship. She doesn't know anything about life. She is too young. It is your responsibility to advise her. You are the experienced person. Advocate reflections: This statement is consistent with an authoritative parent stance. This prioritises the responsibility of the Advocate to advise the younger person on how to think about things and which actions to take, over the student's personal experience. It does not necessarily allow for the student to develop the capacity for personal reflection or choice.

Chorus Three: You need to convince her that she is never going to make it to University. She hasn't the skills. Get her focussed on typing, telephone and writing skills so she can get a job. She needs to face up to reality. Advocate reflections: This approach prioritises the objective realist and calls for the Advocate to prepare the student for something that may not happen. The realist perspective is designed to ensure that the student is prepared for a job, any job but will at least be capable of supporting herself. It is not aspirational.

Chorus Four: You need to be that one person she can trust. She may not have anyone in her world she can trust. You have to be it. Advocate reflections: This statement supports the personal welfare of the student. There is recognition that unless the individual feels a sense of belonging and that there is an adult within the school who cares for them, they may experience personal disconnection and disengagement from school if not life. This statement recognises that school is about personal growth and safety, not only learning.

Chorus Five: You need to get her to the point where she is achieving better in her classes and she won't drop out of school. She is 'at risk' of failing and you're the specific person that can help her. Advocate reflections: This statement reflects the importance of school welfare. It prioritises the responsibility of the school to support the student in their academic skills and achievement, rather than student personal welfare. It may be linked to personal welfare but focuses on curriculum and education to address the issue of risk.

Chorus Six: You need to find out if she has really deep problems that we are not aware of. If you can find those issues that would be great. See if you can dig those out. Advocate reflections: This statement values the psychologically therapeutic approach and is designed to allow the student to reveal her inner most secrets, which are perceived to underpin all the problems the student is manifesting. With some students, psychological therapy may be the only approach to free her from her fears and allow her to engage with life. This often requires a trained practitioner to persuade the student to engage and reveal and to ensure that no psychological harm comes to the student.

Chorus Seven: You need to coach her in how to be compliant with the school culture and then she will find school easier and gain a job after school. This is your responsibility to ensure that she knows how the world works. If you don't do this you are being irresponsible. Advocate reflections: This statement prioritises student compliance to administration and rules. This approach is designed to ensure the student remains in school so they can achieve. If she is already challenging the administration and is resistant, it often requires a 180% change in belief, perception and behaviour on the part of the student. This does not happen quickly, if at all, as she may not see the benefit of an alternative belief to her own. With this view, the school rules appear to be more important than the needs of the student and this may not be her priority.

Chorus Eight: You need to help her with her language skills. They are so poor. This is a great opportunity to correct her skills so she can get a better job. Advocate reflections: This approach is focussed on future job skills. This approach sees Advocacy as a form of one-to-one academic coaching where an expert uses time to redress the deficiencies of the past. If the coaching is based on the student's identification of her own needs and she requests the support, then this may indeed happen in Advocacy. If it is based on the teacher's assessment of the student's needs then it may not be perceived by the student as supportive, but merely judgmental.

Chorus Nine: You need to convince her that eighteen is way too young to be married. Tell her about keeping her options open so she can get a career and make her own choices. Tell her she doesn't have to believe the stories from the 'old country' any more. Advocate reflections: This stance challenges and questions the students' cultural and moral beliefs and behaviours and can prioritise Western beliefs over any other. This may appear to the student to be negative judgment of her, her family and her race and lead to a loss of a sense of belonging and ultimately resistance to learning.

Chorus Ten: You need to give her problem-solving skills so she can be successful in life as well as school. Advocate reflections: This stance prioritises the need for students to have life skills and a way of understanding their world, when adult personal support is lacking. Understanding the processes of learning and how we learn best as individuals can be especially useful if incorporated into the scaffolding provided through classroom teaching.

Each of these chorus voices represent separate, conflicting and complex expectations of the role of an Advocate. As an Advocate it was impossible to meet the expectations of all these teacher voices, together with meeting the needs of students. The chorus spoke from the perspective of adult teachers and their perceptions of what students needed. To undertake Advocacy from this stance would be to duplicate what was already happening in their experience of schooling. What did not often occur was a student-centred approach, where the student voice was listened to, heard and responded to. In undertaking the Advocacy role, I adopted a student-centred approach, offering my support to help students in any way I could, to listen to their stories and concerns, following the principles of Carl Rogers.

ROGERIAN PRINCIPLES: 'WAYS OF BEING' AN ADVOCATE

Although Rogers' work developed from the therapeutic environment and described and explored the elements and attitudes that allowed clients to explore their inner life, he was essentially looking at the qualities of interpersonal relationships and the characteristics of a helping relationship (Rogers, 1980: 39–59).

> By this term I mean a relationship in which at least one of the parties has the intent of promoting the growth, development, maturity, improved functioning, improved coping with life of the other. (Ibid: 40)

It is the purpose of the advocacy relationship to provide a helping relationship for students and encourage schools to incorporate the characteristics of such an environment. Although Rogers' 'necessary and sufficient conditions of therapeutic personality change' (Rogers, 1989) have been widely disseminated, they have often been mistaken in non-therapeutic circumstances as skills or techniques. Teachers in the Advocacy Project initially expressed concern that while they were being asked to establish a helping relationship with students, they lacked the skills, training and experience to counsel students. Therefore, they were provided with Professional Development in basic listening skills and person-centred counselling in order to give them an opportunity to establish and develop helping relationships, following a selection of Rogerian principles.

Instead of focusing on techniques or skills of the counsellor, Rogers has often used the term 'attitude' or a 'way of being'. He is speaking of the subjective experience between human 'becomings' rather than an objective process of expert counsellor with naïve client. The focus upon the subjective functioning of both teacher and student requires both parties to undertake processes of growth, to share the learning between them and to enter into a trusting relationship. Instead of demanding certain techniques or skill of the counsellor or helper, in his work in 'On becoming a person' (1967), Rogers posed questions to encourage reflection. One of his first questions addresses 'Can I be in some way which will be perceived by the other person as trustworthy, as dependable or consistent in some deep sense?' Rogers in his later work referred to this concept as 'congruence' (Wyatt, 2001) but I find his simpler explanation resonates with my experience:

> I have come to recognise that being trustworthy does not demand that I be rigidly consistent but that I be dependably real. (Rogers, 1980: 50)

In Rogers' theory of course, it is not just about the counsellor achieving a feeling of being unified and integrated so that she can be whatever she deeply is. It is about the client perceiving the trustworthiness of the helper. A helping relationship, any relationship, is a two-sided event; if not it is the sound of one hand clapping. Another question Rogers poses is, 'Can I let myself experience positive attitudes toward this other person- attitudes of warmth, caring, liking, interest, respect?' (Rogers, 1980: 52). The wording of this question is intriguing as he uses the term 'can I let myself…' There are notions of granting oneself permission to believe, or act upon attitudes I hold. If I feel positive feelings towards another I may fear that these feelings are not reciprocated or will not be understood by the other or observers.

The next question shows the level of discernment with which Rogers frames these questions. 'Can I permit him to be what he is- honest or deceitful, despairing or over-confident? Can I give him the freedom to be or do I feel that he should follow my advice, or remain somewhat dependent on me, or mould himself after me?' (Ibid: 53). These questions are particularly appropriate to the schooling situation and the role of teacher and helper. In Victoria, the crowded curriculum has ensured that the teacher role has become so much synonymous with judge and expert that the student may rarely experience the teacher as helper. In the teacher role there is also a social imperative towards ensuring that the young are encouraged to conform to the norms of the prevailing culture. The teacher therefore feels pressure to mould the students and channel the student's energy into attitudes and actions that are considered positive. The idea of allowing students to explore their own choices and capacities does not often meet with acceptance within the institutionalised world of the school.

Another question to ask oneself is 'Can I let myself enter fully into the world of his feelings and personal meanings and see those as he does? Can I step into his private world so completely that I lose all desire to evaluate or judge it? Can I enter it so sensitively that I can move about in it freely, without trampling on meanings which are precious to him?' (Rogers, 1980: 53). In later writings Rogers adopted the term 'empathy' to describe this and although I have read and enjoyed these later works and his increasing theoretical complexity, I truly enjoy revisiting the language of these questions as they support me in deeply exploring my subjectivity in ways that theoretical abstraction does not. Although the questions are initially focused upon the helpers' capacity to explore the 'other' it also encompasses the attitude I can adopt towards myself. The notion of accepting the other is encompassed in the questions:

> Can I receive him as he is? Or can I only receive him conditionally, acceptant of some aspects of his feelings and silently or openly disapproving of other aspects? (Rogers, 1980: 54)

Rogers noted here that change does not happen when a person is only conditionally accepted and that generally the non-acceptance has sprung from an attitude of non-acceptance by the helper who has been frightened or fearful of issues presented by the student. If this experience ultimately leads teachers or helpers to self-reflection then they will often discover that it resonates with issues of their own.

Most of these questions centre around the notion of the practicalities of the helping relationship and the role of the helper but Rogers also considered how these aspects will be viewed by the client or, in the case of the advocacy project, the student. 'Can I act with sufficient sensitivity in the relationship that my behaviour will not be perceived as a threat?' (ibid). Students may perceive the schooling environment as an unsafe place where they are constantly being judged against benchmarks that are not of their choosing or even their understanding and therefore feel threatened and afraid of authorities with the power to threaten their achievement. Rogers perceives any negative reaction and feeling of threat as a precursor to disengagement from the helping relationship and so to be avoided.

The previous question is linked to the ninth question of Rogers' list; 'Can I free him from the threat of external evaluation?' (ibid). External evaluation does not promote personal growth as it transfers responsibility onto an external authority figure rather than the personal internal reference. This particular question is the one that is most difficult within a school environment because judgement and evaluation is the basis of the educational experience especially concerning curriculum. Students who perceive the teacher in terms of personal relationship rather than as a conduit of impersonal knowledge transference may not have sufficient discernment to delineate between the teacher's evaluation of their cognitive or academic capacity and a person telling them they are wrong.

The final question that Rogers frames is that which underpins all of the others:

> Can I meet this other individual as a person who is in process of becoming, or will I be bound by his past and by my own past? If I accept him as a process of becoming, then I am doing what I can to confirm or make real his potentialities. (Rogers, 1980: 55)

The thoughts that limit our understanding of the other are so pivotal to education and to the realisation of human potential. The advocacy relationship is an opportunity for students to experience a relationship based on the premises outlined above. Current schooling policies make this difficult to achieve but it makes the intention no less worthy. The subtle underlining of these statements is that we as teachers or helpers are equally exploring our becoming in relationship with the student. It is not only the student who is growing, we are all undertaking this process of becoming. We are not human beings, we are human becomings; it is not a fixed or finished event but an ongoing process. This is the stance I took into my Advocacy role.

STUDENT VOICES OF ADVOCACY

In this section I outline the stories of four students I worked with and how my Advocacy role adapted, as I attempted to meet their varying requirements.

'Junie' was an aspirational Year Ten student. She had indicated early academic promise and was accelerated halfway through the year, from Year 8 to 9. She wanted to be a doctor and believed that her present school was incapable of supporting her to reach her dreams. From me she wanted support for her classes, help with homework, and help to ring private schools to ask about scholarships.

She was tall, willowy with long, dark hair and dark eyes. She was shy and tended to avoid direct eye contact. She had a habit of leaning forwards with a hunched, forward stretching movement of her arms when talking. Here I capture the essence of Junie through a creative reconstruction of her words over several weeks.

Junie

When I was half way through year eight the teachers thought I was really smart and so they promoted me to half way through year 9. They thought I was smarter than the other students. I think I am smarter than other students in this school. They don't study and don't really try hard to do well in exams. I don't think this is a very good school. My mum and her boyfriend think I am smarter than the other students here. Can you ring up private schools for me and find out if they have scholarships?

I need help with my Maths homework. Can you help me with simultaneous equations? Can you help me with Photography homework? Can you help me with Health sciences homework? Health Sciences is boring. All we do is talk about things and the teacher wants us to talk and express opinions. I don't like that. I like it when the teachers tell you what information to gather and the exams are all multiple-choice answers. I like doing that. I get high marks when I do that. I don't like health sciences.

I want to be a Doctor and so I need to do Chemistry class. This school doesn't have Chemistry so I go to TAFE to do it on Tuesday nights. The teacher is horrible because he talks so fast and writes things on the board and then doesn't give us time to write it down. And he keeps talking when we do write it down. I can't understand what he's saying. He talks so fast. Other students have complained too so he's slowed down a bit.

I want to be a Doctor. If you're a Doctor you have an apartment in the City, a nice car and lots of money. I'd like to have an apartment in the City. I don't like blood but I really want to be a Doctor. My mum says I'm smart enough to be a Doctor, so I need to do Chemistry and go to a private school and do medicine at the University of Melbourne. I went to their Open Day and my Mum says they have a really good course.

I have exams coming up soon and I haven't been sleeping very well. I fall asleep in classes sometimes. I know I have to get an A and so I study at home. Other students here don't study. I don't think that this is a good school and I need a good school because I'm brighter than the other students. I think if I went to a private school I'd do better. The students here don't study and the teachers don't make them. It's not a good school. I like being at home with Mum. I don't like being at school. I'm not like the other students. I don't understand just talking in class. The teachers should tell you what they want and how to do it and what they want you to do.

My Advocacy Role with Junie

As a former Secondary teacher I formed opinions of what I thought Junie needed but it would not have been student centred for me to impose them on her, although I was sorely tempted. I also believed in the student-centred process and was committed to trialling it in schools, so I listened and engaged with her and encouraged her to take initiative in developing the skills she was seeking support with. When she asked me to ring the private schools and ask them if they had scholarships, I suggested, consistent with the goal-setting aspect of Advocacy (see Chapter 2) that between us we set a goal, plan how to achieve this and then together we proceed with the ultimate intention of her taking over completely. So she gathered a list of schools, phone numbers, wrote a template of her questions and possible responses, trialled and refined it. Eventually she rang some schools in our sessions and when she felt more confident, she continued the calls at home.

In the Advocacy role that Junie requested, I needed curriculum skills and knowledge to help her develop the capacity to problem solve, and also to encourage her to reflect upon her understanding of her own life requirements, without being judgmental. I undertook this and to a certain extent our interactions were successful. We only met five times and then she finished Year 11 and went to another school. Afternote: Before she left the Advocacy school, she had some problems with staff concerning the validity of her assessment tasks being her own work. The assistant Principal said that Junie and her family had difficulty recognizing that someone else helping her substantially with her work may be seen as unacceptable to the school authorities. The question is moot as to whether her reliance on others may have been addressed if Advocacy had continued for a longer period of time and her personal confidence supported.

Lisa

Lisa was sent to me five weeks before her Year 12 exams, by her teacher, in order for us to apply for TAFE and University courses. She was a quiet, stocky girl of British heritage with mousy coloured, slightly crinkled hair. She was shy at first but believed I was there to help her:

I know I have to do something when I leave school but I don't know what. The teachers tell me I can do a course or go to work. I did work experience for two weeks at an office in Carlton and it was OK but I don't think I want to work there again. The girls were nice but I didn't know what they expected me to do. I think I want to do a course.

I think I might do Nutrition. It sounds good. Someone suggested it and it sounds good. Someone asked me if I like food and if I like to cook and I said I like to cook baked beans when my parents go out. I can look after myself when they go out. I don't know why she wanted to know if I cook.

I might like to do Business, too. I like Business class and I think I'm good at it. My Advocate is showing me the books that describe the University and TAFE courses. I don't understand half of what they are saying. My Advocate described to me what it might be like and this as helpful. I know I have to get this done before the date closes but it's really hard to choose a course. I have put down nutrition, business and hairdressing and I got the forms in on time. I'm glad I got them in because now I can concentrate on my exams.

School is good. I like it. I like the other students and I enjoy coming to school. The teachers tell you what to do and I just do the work. I have done really good to get to Year 12. My sister didn't. And I can go on and do a course after school. The teachers are nice and helpful and I like it here.

My Advocacy role with Lisa would have been more effective if it had started earlier in her schooling, and had begun to develop goal setting skills and career plans in Year 9 or 10. With an Advocate to regularly review her plans with, it would not have been such a shock for her to select further education options without having previously thought about it or researched it in any depth. While she did apply for various courses, I did not hear whether she got into the course she selected.

Matty

Matty was typical of students referred to the Advocacy Program by teachers who assumed it was a problem-solving, quick fix intervention. While Advocacy works best when a trusting relationship has time to be established, this was not the case with Matty, who was in the middle of Year 12 when he was referred to me. He is medium height, slightly heavier than medium weight and wears a cap with the peak facing backwards on his head. He is from a Middle Eastern background and smells of fresh cigarette smoke, although smoking is banned at the school and it is ten in the morning. He sits with his arms wrapped around his shoulders in a self-embrace. He keeps his eyes lowered most of the time, similar to the stance of rap artists he watches on YouTube. It seems that too much eye contact is not cool. His emotions range from frustration to martyrdom:

I am proud of myself. I'm cool and I can prove it by telling you about the things I have done and then you'll know too and maybe get them off my back (gestures towards teachers). I like being who I am, a man who is free to do as I choose. My parents can't control me and I do what I want to do and I like it. I live with them not too far from here and my dad drives me to school. Women and some other men are afraid of me when I walk with my cousin around the building sites, late at night, with his dark blue security jacket and big torch. I wander with him and, by association, I am feared too. I give them a hard look. My cousin tells me that sometimes he carries a gun.

I am also a DJ; I play the music. I know all the latest music. People watch me and admire me. I alone know the music, I alone am allowed in the box with the machines. The one time I've done it was when my aunty invited me to spin the discs for her birthday in Lygon St. I have been a DJ in Lygon St. I am cool. I have made it. Doesn't the school understand that I am cool and that I have made it? They probably don't even know about Lygon St.

On Thursday night I go and watch the guys drag racing on the roads. I don't have a car yet but my parents are going to get me one next year and I'm saving up for the sound system. Then I can drag race with the guys. I can control my car and do burnouts and make loud noises and finger the police and maybe watch the police talk to the cool guys who are doing it. I am cool. I can watch, and smirk and shrug my shoulders into my jacket with all the other guys; watching. We are cool. So I'm late to school the next day. What do they want from me? School is totally uncool. I can't put school over drag racing. None of the other guys do. I am cool.

I sometimes pack fruit at the market. I'm polite and pack the fruit. I get money for this. I can put it towards my sound system. I buggered my back lifting something heavy and I have to take serious painkillers. I'm a real adult now because I've got serious damage to my back and the teachers are worried about me taking painkillers. I can tell and they've told me. They worry about me instead of telling me off. They see me as a cool person; they worry about me. Sometimes. Most of the time they're on my back! They keep wanting me to change; to be what they want me to be. So I miss the Principal's class on a Friday morning and won't pass that subject. Who cares? I don't want to go to University. I want to be a security guard like my cousin and tell people where to go and have them obey me because I have a uniform on; and a torch. And maybe a gun.

I want the teachers to understand that I am an adult and that I make my own decisions. Hanging out with my friends is where I feel like I'm an adult and so at school I like to hang out with friends but I prefer the ones outside school. They treat me like a child here. I want them to treat me like an adult. I work, next year I'll have a car. I am an adult. These subjects, they aren't like real life.

I want to be in real life. In real life you get to feel good, you can make your own decisions and you don't have to do anything if you don't want to. I don't expect much of school. I don't want to be here. I've been here for years and nothing changes. They tell you that you need to do stuff but it doesn't change anything. It's gip. They tell me I have to have my year 12 certificate. Well I'll stay and get that but then I'm outta here. They keep telling you what to do as if you're a kid and get mad if you don't do it. I don't see why I have to do it. It doesn't make any sense to me. They're just on a power trip. They get off on making kids do stuff. Well I'm not going to do it.'

My Advocacy Role with Matty.

I felt as if I was the referee between the school and Matty. Although advocating on Matty's behalf with the school administration was one of my responsibilities, I felt as if decisions has already been made, especially by Matty, who was disengaged from school. He did not appear to understand the school's behavioural expectations or that the intention of school was to educate him and support his progress towards his future. He perceived the teachers as barriers to his desires, rather than as understanding and relational. The Year Level Coordinator reported:

Matty is in Year 12 and he isn't committed to anything really. He knows he needs to get his Year 12 certificate but he isn't happy putting in an effort. He's supposed to attend the Principal's technology class first thing on Friday mornings and he has missed most of them so far this semester. We have spoken to him so many times and he doesn't do anything about it. She, the Principal, is getting furious because he just doesn't care. He says he works late on Thursday night and his Dad can't drive him here on Friday morning and he can't get up early to catch the train. His Aunty lives down the street so we suggest he can stay there on Thursday night and get here early in the morning on Friday but he won't do it. He doesn't really work on Thursdays; he just hangs out somewhere.

He won't get his Year 12 certificate if he keeps going this way and it's such a waste. If he would just attend classes…

Matty did not complete his year 12 certificate and asked for a reference so that he could become a security guard.

IMPLICATIONS OF AN ADVOCACY ROLE

The applications of the Advocacy role are varied, as Advocacy is applied to many different areas within the school environment. As a whole school approach, it could change the school culture from a judgemental, deficit and limited outcome based climate, to a culture that strives for unconditional positive regard, empathy and process based learning. This in turn may have a positive effect on teacher attitudes and student engagement and may prevent student attrition.

The Advocacy Program as it was constructed was an opportunity for school culture to change gradually, because it provided an opportunity for students and teacher/ advocates to meet one-to-one on a regular basis and develop a helping relationship. The relationships formed by the pilot programs in the Advocacy Project allowed dedicated teacher advocates to reflect upon their learning within the relationship and present modelling for such a program within the school and change student/ teacher relating.

It is evident from the research on students 'at risk' that students feel marginalised and disconnected from an early age; they can feel threatened by school, teachers and judgement and they find trusting relationships to be lacking in their lives. Within an Advocacy Program they could share the learning journey together without judgements and build upon the actualising tendency to achieve potentialities. What would ideally happen is that students would find a teacher/advocate with whom they could create a trusting and helping relationship. Having experienced a congruent, empathic and accepting relationship with a teacher within the school, they would find that they were not being judged, drowned in expectations or limited by external benchmarks of behaviour or academic achievement. Building on this, students would develop a sense of self as a person with potential and would develop the capacity to become aware of their own motivations and potential. They would develop the capacity to not rely on external authorities to provide them with reflections on life but their authentic self would emerge from their experience.

In an ideal application of an Advocacy Program, the student/advocate relationship will be perceived by others in the school to be making a discernible and positive difference for the student. Teachers would notice that a helping relationship mitigates against marginalisation and disconnection of students and this awareness would lead to a positive shift in school culture and teacher/student attitudes and relationships. Within these parameters, schools would genuinely understand and adopt a person-centred approach, impacting on teaching and curriculum that would, ultimately, become more student centred.

REFERENCES

Kegan, R. (1998). *In over our heads: The mental demands of modern life*. Cambridge, MA: Harvard University Press.

Rogers, C. (1980). *A way of being*. Boston, MA: Houghton Mifflin Company.

Rogers, C. (1989). The necessary and sufficient conditions for therapeutic personality change. In H. Kirschenbaum & V. L. Henderson (Eds.), *The Carl Rogers reader*. Boston, MA: Houghton Mifflin Company.

Tricia McCann
School of Education
La Trobe University

CAROLINE WALTA AND KIRSTEN HUTCHISON

6. RUNNING IN QUICKSAND

Stories from the Field

THE SCHOOL

Casuarina College* (pseudonym) could be any secondary school, located in an economically depressed rural or regional Australian community, although some schools may have fewer students whose parents are in the lowest SES group. According to the Index of Community Socio- Educational Advantage (ICSEA), during the period of study, over 50% of students at the college were in the lowest quartile, compared to a 25% Australian average, and only 4% in the top quartile. Post school destinations for 2012 indicated that 18% attended university, 24% began TAFE/vocational education, 29% entered employment and 29% were unemployed or not in training or seeking work. Various indicators contributed to the town being identified as one of the most disadvantaged in the state: low school retention rates, high numbers of unskilled workers and adolescent and adult unemployment rates, low per capita income levels, high levels of physical and mental illness leading to frequent emergency medical assistance, high levels of hospital admissions and court appearances.

The Principal

The Principal, a former graduate of the university from which the research team comes, is enthusiastic about making contact with the university again. He is particularly eager to discuss the current crop of problems and challenges facing the school with sympathetic university colleagues. The meeting has been arranged to discuss the possibility of trialling the Student Advocacy Instrument, a set of online tools designed to enhance student learning, welfare and well-being. *(Refer to Chapter 9 for a detailed account of this instrument.)*. The Principal is committed to the principles of advocacy, which he well understands as a relationship of trust and support between individual students and designated staff members. While he is clearly conscious of the benefits of establishing an advocacy program in the school, he is overwhelmed by the demands of his role as Principal, managing 'spot fires' such as fatal car accidents involving students, unhappy and unmotivated staff, angry, uncooperative students, disgruntled parents and the unceasing demands of the Education Department. The Principal laments that approximately 30% of his

K. Hutchison & T. McCann (Eds.), Somebody Knows, Somebody Cares, 69–82.

students can be categorized as "at risk" of early school leaving, by virtue of their location within underemployed families, having low literacy levels, limited social skills and low motivation for remaining at school. They are at risk of perpetuating the circumstances of their own parents. Life for these students and their families is hard. While the Principal is sympathetic to their personal situations and the barriers they face to full participation in schooling and community, currently he has more immediate concerns.

His working day presents challenges which both preoccupy and overwhelm him. They range from the management of new building projects, the oversight of yet another restructure aiming to address the educational needs of his students, issues associated with both natural and private disasters which have profoundly impacted on morale in this school community and a critical mass of staff who feel they are overworked, misunderstood and unsupported in managing the behaviour of the many unruly students. In response to a request to schedule some professional development associated with this program he highlights the nature of his burden:

> We are in regeneration, we are merging two special schools, two primary schools and us onto one site. We have also been applying for all of our special options for a science facility and those sorts of things through the "building revolution" funds... So we have been flat out this term doing that.

He goes on to explain that recent serious bush fires have affected the whole school community directly, with staff and students suffering personal losses and indirectly, with most people knowing families who lost property. The tragic death of a senior student in a road accident had further traumatised the local community:

> Everything that could go wrong has gone wrong. I've just been so busy trying to deal with things... Three years ago it was all flexible learning spaces, now that is out of date and old fashioned, so you need a variety of learning spaces. Most of my staff have taught for thirty years, in classrooms where they teach from the front of the classroom, so they are completely out of their comfort zones.

All this competes for the time of this well-intentioned Principal, who welcomes in theory the idea of an Advocacy Program, but knows that he cannot implement it in the current school climate. What stands in the way of the Principal, doing something to address the needs of students whom he acknowledges as desperately in need of individual help? The decision to amalgamate his school and two other primary schools within one governance system, made without consultation, is purported to be a more efficient and effective way to service the educational needs of students and the community. At the same time, a large scale national building program has been prioritized, requiring his attendance at endless meetings to decide on building designs, budgets and governance of the new amalgamated kindergarten to Year 12 school. He feels justified in his skepticism, since, only a few years ago, he had been directed to establish flexible learning spaces in the school, now this new policy changed the emphasis yet again. Meanwhile, the implementation of the building program is made more difficult by perceived government inefficiency and mismanagement. The amalgamation process requires continual negotiation, shifting positions of responsibility and reallocation of people and resources. He is deeply frustrated by resistance to these changes amongst some of his staff and exhausted by the effort of negotiating every detail of these two initiatives with anxious, stressed staff. Added to this, the implementation of counselling initiatives to support the school community in dealing with the grief and loss of the bush fires also demand his attention, as he attempts to shift the pervasive atmosphere of melancholy present amongst staff and students.

The Principal is distracted by an urgent phone call about a building decision before he can progress the conversation to discuss possible structures of an Advocacy Program for students at risk. He returns to share a further frustration: the quality and dispositions of his teaching staff. He believes that the remote location does not attract quality applicants, with teachers appointed having little idea of contemporary teaching approaches reflecting understanding of pedagogies to address individual needs and student diversity. In general, teachers approach student behavior management in purely punitive terms and their responses to the more open, flexible learning spaces are entirely negative. There are other teachers who unapologetically declare that they 'hate' kids; these he believes, should not be working in schools at all. Most of the staff refuse to undertake any professional learning or further training, which might help to address the multiple complex educational and welfare issues and would rather see new systems or initiatives fail. Of these teachers he notes:

> Well, if you don't want it to work, it won't work. If you won't volunteer to be a home room teacher or if you won't do any training to develop skills and understanding of how to be reasonably nice to the kids, so they co-operate, this again proves that nothing works…

Still he has dreams:

> What we are trying obviously to do, is to get the staff better organized this year so that in a year or two, we will have every kid in our school on an individual learning plan.

Right now however, he does not have the resources to expand the mindset of resistant staff, who reject offers of professional development to investigate alternative teaching and learning approaches. In addition, he bemoans the fact that at Casuarina College, teachers are unwilling to participate in new initiatives without financial incentives, and constrained budgets stretched by building projects do not allow for this.

Miss X: Year 7 Co-ordinator

The Year 7 Co-ordinator is an example of the forms of resistance the Principal faces. Miss X has been teaching for six years and is ambitious to advance in the school system. She is passionate about her subject, English, but is not enjoying the experience at this particular school. She accepted a senior position, which involved year level coordination at a school she knew to be predominately low SES, because it seemed to offer opportunities for promotion. She does not recall learning how to manage these underperforming, disengaged students, many with low literacy, during her university course. However, she has her own ideas about how it should be done, which do not involve rewarding what she perceives as bad behavior, or preparing differentiated tasks to cater for the wide range of abilities and literacy levels in her class. In her view, students should come to class prepared to learn and listen to instructions. If they are frequently absent, there is nothing which can be done to help them, since their families are the problem. According to Miss X, the majority of these students will reproduce their families' cycle of early school leaving, limited training opportunities, unemployment, poverty, and the likelihood of encounters with the legal system.

Miss X is particularly annoyed with the Literacy Support teacher, Mrs A, whose classroom appears to have become a refuge for students whom she regularly evicts from class for a range of offences, mainly involving "unwillingness to work". She has made it quite clear that Mrs A's open door policy is undermining her authority and that exited students are to remain outside her English classroom, without any form of stimulation, as a punishment. When students commit more serious offences, such as verbal abuse or physical violence, she calls for suspension from school. She frequently brings to the attention of parents that their children are not working well in class and is resigned to the perceived lack of parental support she receives. It confirms her belief that these children are destined to reproduce their parents' lives. She is in total disagreement with academic theories and intervention programs which involve making these students feel they are special, or could benefit from an advocate or mentor to present their points of view and address their individual needs. As far as she is concerned, nothing is achieved by not forcing them to conform. She does not feel that she should be doing anything differently in her classes and blames the students and their families for the epidemic of disengagement and underperformance.

RISKY BUSINESS: THE CHALLENGES OF MULTIPLE DISADVANTAGE

In contemporary educational discourses in Australia and internationally, the issue of reducing disadvantage and increasing equity is a recurring topic. Disadvantage is linked in most research to low socio-economic status, remote location, low English language and literacy skills, Indigenous backgrounds and learning difficulties or disabilities. Generally the 'solutions' for addressing disadvantage are conceived in terms of improving initial teacher education, attracting high achieving graduates to teach in 'underperforming' low SES schools, increasing funding for targeted programs to address educational underachievement and retention of particular groups and offering incentives for teachers to work in hard to staff rural and regional locations. (For example, Teach for Australia: http://www.teachforaustralia.org/content/the-problem-of-educational-disadvantage).

Student retention rates are strongly related to school culture with high rates of early school leaving linked to schools characterized by:

* non-stimulating environments with few links to the wider community or the adult world;
* lack of support and referral to appropriate agencies for young people who are experiencing problems in their personal and academic lives; and
* negative teacher/student relationships which are propped up by rules and regulations which disallow young people from expressing themselves as adult and responsible members of the school community (Innovation and Best Practice in Schools: DETYA 2001).

However, there is agreement that the solution to disengagement lies in the redefinition of learning experiences along personalised or student-centred lines. Student-centred learning underpins the practice of the comparatively few schools internationally that combine high student poverty with high achievement. These schools have a challenging curriculum that is connected to students' lives and to the community in which they live; that presents authentic tasks requiring complex thought and allowing time for exploration; that caters for individual differences in interest and learning styles; that develops cooperation, communication, negotiation and social competencies generally; and that emphasises depth of understanding and control over one's learning (Centre for Applied Educational Research, 2002; Kannapel & Clements, 2005; Walsh & Black, 2009; Black, 2007).

The term 'students at risk' describes a category of students who are at risk of failing to complete school for a range of reasons, some of which are more readily addressed than others. (Please refer to *Chapter 3 Backgrounding Advocacy* for further information.) There is ample evidence, both anecdotally and in research that the system is failing a significant number of students. These students are more likely to be found in rural and low-socioeconomic suburban schools in Australia. Here we see lower than average literacy scores, higher dropout rates and multi-generational unemployment being factors, in some centers. Schools proliferate with structures to support students at risk and address disadvantage: school counsellors, chaplains, social workers, case managers, level coordinators, literacy support personnel to name a few. School building projects are underpinned by good intentions, to support better learning outcomes for students. School personnel are beset with directives, which demand accountability for achievement. Why is this system still failing?

Glasser's 'choice theory' (Glasser, 1997) offers one explanation, with its' insistence on the notion of self-management and the understanding that the only behavior we can control is our own. Glasser's work offers a theoretical framework for examining disadvantage in the context of self-management and student wellbeing. While there is significant research evidence suggesting that problems of disadvantage and alienation can usefully be addressed through the lens of theories about student well-being, examples of successful integration of these understandings into whole school programs is not well documented. Glasser's theory proposes the notion that humans are driven by four psychological needs: the need to belong, the need for power, the need for freedom and the need for fun. The concept of a 'quality world' is linked to needs, as we identify with people who we see as supportive of our needs, people who are perceived to care and who are cared for by us in return. School climates in which teachers are unable to cultivate a sense of personal empowerment and belonging in their students, where the freedom to learn in a creative environment is compromised, are likely to be resisted. For the students we will introduce in the next section of this chapter, schools and teachers are largely absent from their quality worlds. Glasser's theory strongly supports the notion of positive relationships in the management of students at risk. Further, it suggests that suggest that the extreme, personal and multilayered disadvantage experienced by many students at risk requires a relationship-based approach. This will support student initiative and cultivate choices, which will enhance rather than destroy their options for self-improvement through education. (For more on Glasser please refer to *Chapter 3: Backgrounding Advocacy*.)

This chapter records the experience of one of the authors, a university academic who, as part of a team of researchers, was exploring the use of a set of online tools, the Student Achievement Inventory (SAI), a database of electronic questionnaires, designed to support students to reflect on their learning and plan educational pathways (See Chapter 9 *Using Digital Data to Support Student Engagement*). A number of schools in rural and regional Victoria were trialling this program, together with professional development for staff, provided by the university, in advocating for students. Students participating in this program were given access to a range of questionnaires, through which they would record information about their challenges and aspirations in association with their involvement in schooling and together with their teacher – advocates, would set goals for improving their learning behaviours and general well-being. Only one staff member, the Literacy Support teacher, Mrs A, expressed interest in being involved, motivated by an increasingly desperate search for an effective response to the numbers of students entering secondary school from primary schools, who were at risk of under achievement and early exit from secondary education, due to the lack of structured and effective support programs. The students' limited literacy and numeracy skills, low self-esteem, highly reactive behaviours and propensity to disconnect from classroom activities highlighted the school's failure to address their complex social, emotional and educational needs.

In the remainder of this chapter, we introduce some of the individuals forming this school community, visited by one of the university researchers over a two year period. We illustrate how the situation described, is not caused by lack of awareness of the issues confronting students at risk, but by misdirected management and ineffective pedagogical approaches. Student management becomes mismanagement when coercive discipline is the choice of strategy for disadvantaged students. If students at risk cannot perceive goodwill in their relationships with teachers at school, they are likely to be wary of any teacher initiated programs which require mutual trust and respect, despite benevolent overall aims of developing insight into their own learning behaviours and increasing their capacity and motivation to learn.

SOMEBODY CARES: THE SAFE HAVEN OF MRS A'S CLASSROOM

There was one teacher who saw things differently: Mrs A, the literacy support person, previously introduced. She knew significantly more about the needs of individual students than almost any other teacher, in part because of her role to meet with teachers from feeder primary schools, in order to identify and understand the histories and circumstances of students who may require individualized support to achieve a successful transition into secondary education. This enabled her to identify students potentially at risk of underachievement and disengagement and begin to understand the complex factors impacting on their capacity to fully participate in schooling. This knowledge informed her student-centred literacy pedagogy, providing targeted literacy support across the curriculum, to small groups and individual students. According to many students interviewed during the research, she was the only person at the school who was approachable, who appeared to care about them individually, as people. By default, Mrs A became an advocate for all students requiring literacy support and for those who sought her out. Unfortunately in deputizing for these students, in trying to explain why a certain student was unsettled or disruptive, she positioned herself in opposition to the rest of the staff, someone to be ignored or criticized, because she was perceived to support and excuse bad behaviour.

At a given point in the school day, an observer might see Mrs A working with a group of young teenagers, probably Year 7, giving individualized, support to students in literacy and numeracy skills. Her room is something of a refuge for other students. A regular deputation of exited students rap on her door, asking to be allowed to come in, as they have been sent out from another class, for 'bad behaviour' of some sort. Mrs A struggles to conceal her frustration with her colleagues, as she welcomes the students and attempts to provide a safe haven for these academically struggling students. This often sets her in conflict with the exiting staff member, who has expressly forbidden that the behavior be 'rewarded' with time out with the supportive Mrs A. This situation seems un-resolvable as often, the teacher expelling students from her class is the Year 7 coordinator herself, who has overall responsibility for student welfare. Students routinely attempt to explain how it came about that they were asked to leave the class, a regular occurrence that too often affirms a belief that they are disliked and therefore unfairly treated.

Mrs A is uncertain about the benefits of online questionnaires, aimed at helping students to identify their skill sets, goals and learning needs in various subjects. Her problem is that most students with whom she works have such low reading skills that they cannot fully access the material. Furthermore their learning needs

75

are so idiosyncratic in her view, that no questionnaires could provide meaningful information about them. Their stories will be subsequently told. She explains how she has to seek opportunities to see some students during home group time, which was supposedly for administration. For example, she voluntarily mentored one student, Trudy, during that time, to ensure she complied with court orders to keep her in school and off the streets:

> The advocate work there was related to her court case, so we developed a program and that meant that every morning I went to her Home Room to check whether she was there. If she wasn't at school, I phoned home or went walking and looking for her, so that was a very intensive use of time.

Trudy was one of approximately 15 children with whom Mrs A had a personal, caring relationship throughout one year. Checking that they were actually at school was the first priority and involved her in moving from home group to home group each morning. Truancy for these at-risk students was high and her goal for several of the children was to ensure that they didn't drop out altogether and join the street gangs. Invariably these students entered secondary school with very poor literacy skills and were in need of extensive in class support. Mrs A identified that 30% of children entering Year 7 were moderately or severely at risk. No specific structures were in place to deal with the needs of these students on an individual basis, other than her work in numeracy and literacy support. She first had to win over their trust:

> Very quickly they realize that I'm not there to interfere with their lives, that I am there to make their lives easier at school, because the whole focus is what can we do at school to make things work better for you?

While Mrs A's official role was literacy support, she voluntarily met with students who sought her assistance and attempted to advocate for them, with a largely hostile staff, and with welfare agency representatives, who were often, in her opinion, disconnected from and in extreme cases vindictive, towards children in their care.

Because Mrs A felt that supporting these students' academic needs was a challenge she addressed almost single handedly, she welcomed the collegiality of the university research team. A number of students under her care were functionally illiterate. All underperformed in literacy, especially in comprehending written texts, due to limited vocabulary and oral language. The development of social and communication skills was another priority, given the frequent conflicts they had with other students and staff. According to Mrs A, the self-monitoring of school attendance and tracking of achievement of personal goals was a valuable feature of the SAI for these students, however low literacy skills prevented them from using these features without individual assistance, which was time consuming to manage. Her preference was for each student to have their own advocate:

> I think it is really important that the child has an adult who can advocate for them at school and at home. It gives the child a buffer. If a child can experience

that non-judgmental, trusting relationship it's teaching them how to relate in later life to lots of situations.

Sadly this is not seen as a role for the home group teachers, who perform only administrative functions:

Secondary schools have children going to lots of different teachers. Unless at risk students are fortunate enough to be connected to the school's welfare or pastoral care programs, it's unlikely they'll develop trusting relationships.

Individual students may be in detention or suspended and missing a great deal of class time, which no one is monitoring. She feels that what is needed is acceptance of where a child is and for someone to make school work for a child. According to Mrs A, the core business of schooling is:

Working out how to make learning happy, in a safe and calm environment. We have so many behaviour problems because kids are really saying 'NOBODY CARES AND LIFE IS TOO HARD.'

In the following section, we introduce some of the students who sought sanctuary in Mrs A's classroom.

The Students: Portraits of Disconnection

Thalia and Cassie[1]

Mrs A was deeply concerned about two students Cassie and Thalia, who began their secondary schooling system with a history of underachievement at primary school and were unable to fully participate in classroom activities due to low levels of literacy. They were seldom in class, since teachers regularly evicted them before they could sit together and "make trouble," generally by talking. The 13 year old friends, were already at risk of dropping out of school due to feelings of alienation. Cassie, who lived with her mother and step father, intensely disliked school, because she felt most teachers "picked on" her, sent her out of class for "nothing," with no warning and didn't care about her. Consequently, she was unmotivated, learnt little and rarely received the additional support she needed to understand the work. Thalia, who lived with her mother and three siblings, also felt unfairly targeted and misunderstood by her teachers. Her mother insisted that getting a good education was her daughter's only chance, but did not know how to initiate a conversation with teachers about her daughter's aspirations and her perceptions of unfair treatment by teachers. The girls were friends, despite their awareness that being together antagonized their teachers.

In a series of interviews with one of the researchers, the girls eagerly presented their point of view, that the Year 7 coordinator appeared to be their main barrier to learning. While they agreed that sitting together possibly antagonized teachers, as they conferred with one another in an attempt to understand what was required, their perception was that teachers did not seem to consider it their responsibility to help them access set work. They tried a strategy of entering classrooms quietly, sitting apart, then asking the teacher for help to begin tasks, but invariably, before long, they were sent out for a previous misdemeanor. Thalia and Cassie were perceived as troublemakers, in part because their literacy skills were so limited that they were unable to work at the expected level without individualized instruction. Perhaps if they had been offered targeted, expert assistance and positive reinforcement from their teachers, they could have made progress. Without compassion, understanding or accommodation of their situation by their teachers, these girls were effectively excluded from learning at school.

Jaxon

12 year old Jaxon described a complex family situation: 12 siblings, living with different foster families, while Jaxon himself lived with his elderly grandparents, who loved and cared for him, but had limited energy to devote to his interests and multifaceted needs. His mother, sadly, had become addicted to illegal and prescription drugs and disappeared when he was 5 years old:

I don't have contact with my mum…sometimes I wonder where she is.

Other students teased him because of his family situation, and he was regularly provoked into playground fights, leading to frequent suspensions from school. Mrs A worked with Jaxon on literacy and numeracy, conscious of his many challenges, and he was grateful for her help and concern. His welfare case worker appeared harsh and disinterested in his emotional health. For example, Jaxon's red hair incited continual bullying and teasing. When he dyed his hair to escape the torment from his peers, his case worker angrily ordered him to restore his natural colour, without attempting to address the bullying he was subjected to. By contrast, his ongoing relationship with Mrs A offered comfort and helped him deal with the teasing and bullying. However, she was usually busy and at times it was difficult to find a private time to speak with her, especially when other teachers specifically forbade him from going to her room and instead sent him to the Principal or Year Level Head, for a dose of discipline.

Abby

Like Jaxon, despite an extended family of nine sisters and three brothers, Abby was the only child living with her mother and a step parent. She struggled to speak and had very low level literacy skills. She needed individualized academic support to manage classroom tasks but was unmotivated to undertake anything resembling school work. She was reluctant to get out of bed in the morning, but her mother forced her to attend:

Most days I don't like it and I don't really want to be there and I don't take in what they [teachers] say.

She had several pets at home, but was reluctant to walk the unregistered dogs. Although Abby enjoyed sport, especially running, she was unmotivated to train or join any of the school teams. Abby had multiple special needs which had not been addressed throughout her primary schooling and without the specialist, individual support she needed, Abby was effectively excluded from most of the learning experiences at school.

Tyrone

Tyrone, 15, was facing serious trouble: a potential conviction for assaulting another student in the school-yard. When Tyrone was 6 years old, his father took his own life. He was haunted by this memory. He had not received appropriate counseling or support after the tragic death of his father and was left alone to manage as best he could, with low literacy levels and an enduring sense of failure. In the strange climate of social dysfunction he inhabited at school, other students teased him about the loss of his father. On one such recent occasion, as he was playing basketball at lunch time, a boy became angry over an umpiring decision and insulted Tyrone about his father. Although he had ignored many similar insults, this time, momentarily enraged, he punched and kicked the boy until he was unconscious. Tyrone remembered finally stopping and taking the boy's pulse, alarmed that he might have hurt him. He hoped that the courts would acknowledge his genuine remorse and allow him to continue with his schooling somewhere else, as he wanted to further his secondary education and ultimately join the army. He had been making progress this year with Mrs A and was finally becoming a more competent reader. Tyrone was also committed to ensuring that his peers and the school community respected the memory of his father.

Unlike the other student portraits presented, Tyrone's story had a happy ending. Mrs A asked the researcher, who was visiting the school that day to conduct research interviews, to write Tyrone an additional character witness statement for the courts, in the hope that this might prevent the imposition of a custodial sentence in a juvenile justice centre. The magistrate accepted both character witness statements from the researcher, and Mrs A and allowed him to live with a relative in another town and continue his education at a school there. Given that Tyrone was already under total and permanent expulsion from the school when he was invited to participate in the research interview, the intervention of Mrs A was both remarkable and timely. Her sensitivity and compassion made it possible for Tyrone to share his story with another well-respected adult, a university researcher, who ultimately was willing and able to advocate for him as a character witness. The caring and targeted support of this teacher undoubtedly changed the direction of his life, in offering him a much needed second chance at education.

In this instance, both Mrs A and the research team were asking the same questions: who are the students 'at risk,' what are their individual needs and how can teachers and schools foster their learning? Both Mrs A and the research team were convinced of the centrality of strong relationships between students and teachers to powerful learning.

However, the incentive to work with such students was diminished for many teachers at the school, within the general competitive, insecure workplace environments where teacher performance is assessed in terms of increases in student achievement and school rankings, based on standardized national testing. Further, the 'overwhelming needs' of students in schools like Casuarina place enormous demands on formal and informal communication channels, in terms of collating and sharing information about individual students, classroom incidents, academic progress, health and welfare issues. Without user friendly information systems and rapid communications in place, teachers did not have access to the personal situations of individual students which were essential to inform the interpersonal relationships on which day to day teaching was grounded. Mrs A was at times overwhelmed by the complexity of her work, and felt exhausted and undervalued. She was convinced of the efficacy of student-centered teaching practices for increasing student engagement and confidence in learning and for strengthening positive relationships between teachers and students and thus minimizing disruptive behavior. The school was located in an economically depressed region, with inadequate access to networks of skilled professional able to support the work of educators, such as psychologists, counsellors, social workers, youth workers. Assisting students to navigate the difficult territory of schooling and access forms of cultural and social capital which were not available to them within their families and communities fell to Mrs A and too few of her colleagues. In this school context, a significant proportion of both teachers and students were overwhelmed by the demands upon them.

CONCLUSION

There are multiple players in these brief case studies of the children and their teachers at Casuarina College: teachers trained to teach their subjects, anxious about their job security and the limited ways in which their professional competence is measured in relation to student performance on standardized tests. Punitive, competitive school policies, scarce resources and adequate infrastructure place huge demands on teachers working in such locations of high poverty. While there are numerous programs, schemes and organizations working to address disadvantage, still too many students fail or disengage, leaving school with limited opportunities for further educations, employment or training. Supporting students with such complex academic, social, physical and emotional needs is challenging, demanding and exhausting labour. In these environments, despite good intentions, some students can be viewed as 'too hard': those who are underachieving academically, often due to the failure of their primary education to establish foundation literacy and numeracy, these students are likely to experience generational unemployment and cycles of entrenched poverty. Sadly, there are many similar stories particularly in rural areas, where there are limited opportunities for employment and viable pathway options into further education & training. In school communities such as Casuarina, precious teacher energy is often consumed by behavior management of kids struggling to survive, socially, academically, emotionally, leaving little time or inclination to recognize the many positive qualities and sets of knowledge these students possess.

This chapter is a tribute to the work of teachers such as Mrs A, who are willing to take on challenging students and demonstrate through their compassion that one caring, empathetic, skilled teacher can make a difference. As Nel Noddings emphasizes, caring relations are the foundation for pedagogical activity:

> First as we listen to our students, we gain their trust and, in an ongoing relation of care and trust, it is more likely that students will accept what we try to teach...Second, as we engage our students in dialogue, we learn about their needs, working habits, interests and talents. We gain important ideas from them about how to build our lessons and plan for their individual progress. Finally, as we acquire knowledge about our students' needs and realize how much more than the standard curriculum is needed, we are inspired to increase our own competence. (Noddings, 2010: 3)

Schools need to value teachers such as Mrs. A and offer sustained, relevant professional learning in how to relate to, support and teach students at risk of underachievement and disconnection from learning. The challenges of improving life chances for students in disadvantaged communities are vast and complex; adequately resourcing the development of sustainable, tailored, school-wide programs to expand the capacities of teachers, schools and communities to care and advocate for equity is one step forward.

NOTE

[1]   All student names are pseudonyms.

REFERENCES

Black, R. (2007). *Crossing the bridge: Overcoming entrenched disadvantage through student-centred learnin*. Melbourne, Australia: Education Foundation.

Centre for Applied Educational Research. (2002). *Middle Years Research and Development (MYRAD) project executive summary* (February–December, 2001). A report to the learning & teaching innovation division, department of education & training. Melbourne, Australia: The University of Melbourne.

Clegg, S., & Rowland, S. (2010). Kindness in pedagogical practice and academic life. *British Journal of Sociology in Education, 31*(6), 719–735.

Department of Education, Training and Youth Affairs. (2001). *Innovation and best practice in schools*. Victoria Government.

Glasser, W. (1997). A new look at school failure and school success. *Phi Delta Kappan, 78*(6), 597–602.

Henkel, M. (2000). *Academic identities and policy change in higher education.* London, UK: Jessica Kingsley.

Kannapel, P. J., & Clements, S. K. (2005). *Inside the black box of high performing high poverty schools.* Lexington, Kentucky: Prichard Committee for Academic Excellence.

Noddings, N. (2010). *Caring in education.* Retrieved June 24, 2014 from http://www.infed.org/biblio/noddings_caring_in_education.htm

Skelton, A. (Ed.). (2007). *International perspectives on teaching excellence in higher education: Improving knowledge and practice.* London, UK: Routledge.

Walsh, L., & Black, R. (2009, October 2–4). *Overcoming the barriers to engagement and equity for all students,* Paper presented at Australian curriculum studies association 2009, Biennial conference curriculum: A national conversation, Canberra.

Caroline Walta
Faculty of Education
Latrobe University

Kirsten Hutchison
Faculty of Arts and Education
Deakin University

KIRSTEN HUTCHISON AND DON COLLINS

7. YOU CAN'T DO ADVOCACY FOR
15 MINUTES A DAY

Whole School Approaches to Advocacy and Mentoring

This chapter presents a dialogue between a university based researcher and a secondary school principal about the power of advocacy and mentoring programs in defining and shaping school cultures. It describes the importance of whole-school approaches to advocacy and mentoring programs, outlines key organisational features and details the transformative effects on students, staff and school culture.

Kirsten: *To begin with, tell me what distinguishes Coburg Senior High School from other schools?*

Don: Coburg Senior was setup with a real purpose in mind and that was about educational provision in the north at that particular point in time, back in 2006, when I came on board as Principal.

There'd been a steering committee that had been set up, comprised of people from the centre, local community members, local principals etc, people from the regional office, to get the thing going and then bring in a principal, whoever it might be, to create the reality. So I came in with a mandate to do it differently. I didn't have to deconstruct, just restructure. Our aim was to produce good student learning outcomes, infusing ICT through everything we do. There was a focus on good academic results and a breadth of curriculum, but also the mandate to actually create learning for the connected generation, and essentially that's what we've done. Everything was set up around having flexible pathways for students, to actually have a work component to our programs, so the vocational part was as important as the academic. So in our first year for example, we had every student in the school out on work placement doing a Vocational Education Certificate (VET) in the first year. People saw it as an experimental school because we weren't using text books, all those sorts of things just add to the particular challenges. But the theory was: we're going to use technology, we're going to integrate, yes you can bring your mobile phone, no there's no uniform but there's a dress code and this is about getting great academic results. To do this, we knew that we had to build a school where there was a real sense of

K. Hutchison & T. McCann (Eds.), Somebody Knows, Somebody Cares, 83–95.

connection, where we would know the students really well and find ways we could connect with them through an advocacy model, which I'd been introduced to in 1998.

Kirsten: *And what did you see the potential was then, why did it stay with you?*

Don: I think it's because … in order to get the best out of a student you really need to know who they are … I think this is a key thing, students need to feel connected to their school and to the people who work with them. If you don't know them, you can't actually work out what they really need on an academic level. So differentiating and understanding the skills sets they already have and the gaps in their learning and where we need to develop them. How do we give it back to them in a way that makes a difference? I can teach you a fantastic lesson, but if you don't learn anything from it then what's it worth? So it's about making sure that the quality of teaching and learning recognises the need to differentiate and recognise their strengths.

As an example, in the first where we had some Technical and Further Education (TAFE) teachers year come in and teach a particular component they rocked up with thirteen text books and walked in to the learning area, stood at the front desk and said, "Right, take a book each and open up to chapter 13 and do the first three questions," and our kids just sat there and said "I don't think so."

Kirsten: *So they had enough agency to say, this is not going to work for us, we're not doing it.*

Don: Yeah, they were saying, "We're not here to do this, we're here because we know we need something better than we've been given." That is a common thread in our students, who have voluntarily decided in Year 8 or 9, I want to leave my mates and my school and come to somewhere different.

The other challenge for the school is we've never had feeder school. Students who apply to come here have to be brave enough to make the move, so their sense of agency is quite strong. The enrolment processes is such that you have to enrol online, have an interview that goes anywhere from 45 minutes to an hour and a half sometimes. You have to bring in your last 3 semester reports, you've got to bring your NAPLAN data, and we have a conversation about pathways and suitability and commitment and transparency. And students become really keen. You just can't rock up, fill out a form, and go "Oh, I'm in."

Kirsten: *So as a potential student you have to articulate your needs, desires, aspirations, to someone who is going to be able to help you presumably.*

Don: As I often say, we don't care what your pathway is, so bricklayer or astrophysicist is fine, you can choose either. What's important is you can start off wanting to be an astrophysicist or a bricklayer and end up being a musician, but you should be able to have flexibility and a pathway to be able to change your mind. Of course there's a point where you do have to commit to a particular pathway. Part of is knowing what do you need to do in order to become an astrophysicist, a scientist, or an event manager. If you don't have a goal, well you don't have an eye on a prize, then how can you know why you need to better at maths, why you need to be better at accessing language and processing it and what it means to you in terms of your employability. But it's that knowing, which is really, really important. So you can say to kids, "You're actually crew, you're not a passenger." Marshal McCluhan said "There are no passengers on this space ship, only crew." That's the concept. One of the reasons why I keep Kurt Hahn over there on my window there, in the frame*,

> ** I regard it as the foremost task of education to ensure the survival of these qualities: an enterprising curiosity; an undefeatable spirit; tenacity in pursuit; readiness for sensible self-denial; and above all COMPASSION. Kurt Hahn*

That's what we're trying to do without being involved in an outward bound course. You know teaching students sensible self denial. That they've got to be curious cause we've done a fantastic job in education of beating the curiosity out of kids.

So it's about teaching them their obligation and their responsibility to be an active participant.

Kirsten: *I think this leads on really nicely to this idea of the mentor group models. Can you talk about what they are and how you think they impact on the culture of the school and on student learning and on teachers' understandings of what teaching is?*

Don: We've had several iterations of the mentor model. Initially, it occurred before school, at lunch times or recess because we were small enough to be able do that. Then we worked out rotating times, Now, it's time tabled for 75 minutes every week, and that mentoring period is only one part of it, so mentoring is built into teachers' loads, not an addition. There's an acknowledgement that there's lots of mentoring that's happening outside that time, but within that time you might be doing all the different forms of Social Education: Drug Ed, Sex Ed, Study Ed, all the elements...

Kirsten: *...life skills.*

Don: Life skills, then it's about communication and it's about also attendance, notes, and other organisation logistics and then going for walk. Staff have actually worked out that going for a walk in Mentor Group can be really good, because there's lots of really good conversations that can happen when you walk, rather than sitting round a table and talking to kids.

Kirsten: *Yeah, not looking at each other, you're moving, you're a bit relaxed...*

Don: Yeah, so it's kind of like, "What's going on with maths at the moment, some issues blah, blah, blah... And also there's the transparency of communicating as a staff, because we use an online system. So we could be out in the yard and you're a student and I'm a teacher and there's an issue. I don't know let's say, about some rubbish on the ground that you've thrown and didn't want to pick it up, going back to that sort of junior school reality. I can have a discussion with you where you end up picking it up, or you could actually decide you want to dig your heels in because you claim it's not yours, even though I watched you throw it on the ground type scenario. Well you get to choose in terms of how that gets dealt with, but ultimately I can come back in and log on next time in front of them, and describe the incident day, this happened, blah, blah, press the button, it goes to the mentor. So I don't have the conversation as I pass the mentor in the corridor, "Oh by the way..." It's logged and it's available and the mentor gets a flag that says there's a note for you, see what happened. So there's accountability, transparency, finding ways to communicate back, so that the mentor can either follow it up straight away if needed, or they might decide next time we go for a walk, I'm going to talk to x about that.

Kirsten: *What about in terms of students learning, how does the mentor relationship act as a fulcrum for learning?*

Don: It's difficult being an adolescent isn't it really? You've got so many things going on, so many issues to resolve and work out. Once again, if they don't feel connected, if they don't feel safe, if they don't feel listened to, if they don't feel as if they've got a voice, then they become unsettled in most things and then they're not efficient in their studies. You need to know what's going on with a student, you need to have someone who is sending you the message, or saying, "Look, there's some issues for Don at home. As Don's mentor, I know that something's going on, so you need to cut him a bit of slack at the moment. He may be irrational, but it's not you, it's him, processing stuff." It could be about mental health issues. It could be about body issues. It could be about all sorts of things, but someone needs to know and therefore communicate it, so the staff have got a better idea. Because if you don't know that's going on and you're really getting frustrated with them about the work they're not doing, and discover that their grandmother passed away last week, but you didn't know, all those sorts of things are really important in Advocacy. Someone knows those students really well and can act and pass on information. That's powerful in terms of how you handle a kid, because as an educator in a classroom with of students, you're busy trying to work out how you're going to massage the situation in the right way so you get the best possible outcome.

In schools where the teachers have weak or negative relationships with their students, there are the greatest number of problems; the data is overwhelming. Teachers need to know where and how their students are in order to get the best out of them. So for us as a school, the Advocacy model is all about making sure we know who our students are. So information is shared electronically, so that the appropriate multiple people immediately know there's an issue with student A, B, C, or D. Everyone knows that Jack opened the United Nations Speech in parliament last week, so if you see him, make sure you acknowledge this. It's not all about the negative, it's about sharing all the positive, great things. There are staff at performances, sporting events who see their students doing really well. Now teachers are busy, I'm not asking them to work 20 hours a day, but it's about encouraging everyone to attend a least a couple of events each year, so they can have that conversation with a kid. Who knew that Aamir was a fantastic tabla drummer, and that he can sing beautifully in Arabic? Who knew that Eliza, who came in hating dance, suddenly picked up dance, and now here's Eliza, starring in the dance performance last night. If you're not part of that experience you can't use it as an opportunity for conversations.

Kirsten: *Absolutely. So how do you support, teach, expand teachers' notions of their responsibilities, the possibilities inherent in teaching? Clearly not everyone arrives equipped for that kind of complex work, beyond what they might see as their primary aim to teach content.*

Don: If you think that's your prime job, you shouldn't be here, because I would argue that teaching content is not the prime responsibility of educators in today's market.

Your job is to have breadth, depth and passion for your subject, so that you can sell it to kids, share it in engaging ways, but your job is so much more than that. This is a profession; you have to be able to provide an educational experience that works, that is comprehensive, that enables students, with all the complex issues they may have, to be successful, confident and competent. Staff go through an induction program and then it's about constant conversations.... For example, let's choose Sex Education; some staff are really uncomfortable talking about sexual relationships. We always bring experts in from outside to do some of the specialist elements and then we pair staff together, so someone who's uncomfortable with someone who's totally comfortable, and they then together engage in conversations with the students. So it's about knowing the staff support that needs to be put in...

Kirsten: *So it's mentoring the mentors?*

Don: Every teacher has a leading teacher/principal class mentor, who they can ask: "What am I meant to do here? What needs to be followed up? I've tried everything with this kid, where do I go to next?" There's a structure in place to support teachers, because they are the key adults, the educators, people with the life experience to deal with students who have a whole range of needs. It's the mixed ability classroom reality on every level, not just the academic...

Kirsten: *Can you talk a bit more about how the professional action inquiry teams work as part of the advocacy and mentoring philosophy, to collaboratively investigate issues that arise?*

Don: There's a constant intention to continually build relationships with the kids, to maximise their learning ... knowing there's always another technique or thinking strategy that might be applied, finding different ways to understand how individual kids learn. So action inquiry teams in the school have always asked: What do we want to explore? What are the critical questions now? What are our theories of action? What are we reading? What can we then apply in the classroom? What do we need to review in our a small groups of staff? How can we showcase what we've learnt to the rest of the staff?

Kirsten: *So how are the action inquiry teams put together?*

Don: Once again several versions over the years. In our first year we had 13 ideas we wanted to explore, which was reduced to 6 and staff elected to go into whatever they were most interested in. That's been the way it works with different kinds of leadership. Situational leadership is really strong in the school, so we've had an early career teacher leading one of those action inquiry teams, even though there was a leading teacher and an experienced teacher in the same team. It was about who wants to have the opportunity, what will they learn and what will be the value for them and the school? This year, all the action inquiry teams are led by expert teachers and that's connected to a new work agreement, where you need to do what's commensurate with your level and we thought okay we're going to reformat that this year. But it's still that notion of choosing which team you'd like to be involved in and getting a balance of who is in what team and that kind of naturally kind of happens.

Kirsten: *And so what kind of questions are people exploring this year?*

Don: Well it's about data driven improvement and an online focus. We're trying to thread literacy and effective use of ICT all the way through our action inquiries and create digital resources and digital assessment tools and practices. Staff members can provide a formative comment on the work a student's doing on the wiki, because their workspace is the wiki. Or I can write a note on the wiki about a student as a classroom teacher that's just for me, or I can send it to the student, or to the parents, or I can put this comment on the end of term report. I have all those capacities. When I send the note to the parent and the student, they get an SMS with a descriptive assessment, so it's a call to action for the parent to go and look for the rest of the data on line, access the link to the rubric and to the link to the actual work on the wiki, so they actually get to see an assessment in the context of the task. And the student gets the SMS as well and says oh, man the folks know this. Okay…

Kirsten: *…I'd better get my story right.*

Don: Exactly right. But we also want parents to celebrate the work of their kids, and also to know what they're doing. Oh, so you're doing this stuff in physics, do you know crusty old Bill across the road is a retired professor from the University of Blah, you should go and talk to him.

Kirsten: *So connecting the out of school resources with the in school worlds?*

Don: I'm not suggesting that happens with every parent and every student, every time, but you can create the potential for that to happen. Because you know around the world the conversation between parents and students run like this: "How was school today?" "Yeah good". "Have you got any homework?" "No".

When clearly they do. And OK, parts of the day were good, but what parts of it were bad? Parents can just look on the wiki and say, "That work you're doing on the fulcrum of the shadoof and Egypt and ancient times is actually quite complex isn't it? It reminds me about boomerangs. Do you realise how powerful boomerangs are? Blah, blah, blah, suddenly there's dialog between parents as opposed to "Oh yeah good, no, nothing."

Kirsten: *And also a potential power shift as well.*

Don: Yes. It also illustrates another central tenet of the school which is about co-learning. Anyone can be an expert on stuff. I remember a few years ago we had some boys who were into street art and skate boarding. We offered them the opportunity to lead a unit of work on graffiti and street art. So the kids in that class went to the city, took photographs of all of the graffiti and street art they liked, geo-mapped it on a Google map and sent it to the City of Melbourne and asked, "Did you know this is where all the graffiti is?" For some of them it was the first time ever in their school careers they initiated something, they shared their knowledge and they were teaching their peers and their teachers. That's a great example of what can happen, as opposed to, "I'm the teacher, I know, and I'm going to drip feed you the information you need." Those days are gone.

Kirsten: *It's clear that the digital connectedness you embrace at the school is critical in opening up learning opportunities. It's an interesting model of professional learning to invite staff to develop a collaborative narrative about what they think is going on, and how they might do it differently? What does the leadership group need to know then in order to help make this happen?*

Don: I think I'll answer that by saying, if you go to my Twitter account my by-line says, "Reflection equals revolution." You must make time for everyone to stop and reflect and ask, "How is it going and why is it so?" You've got to allow everyone in the learning community to stop and reflect, because that allows a revolution to take place. For some people it's an epiphany, for others it's thinking about what we need to be asking in order to know there's a problem, or whether this worked really well, or if something needs to be developed. You've got to stop and think and reflect and there are a whole lot of strategies we use, including positive psychology. We need to ensure that students and staff have got the right inner voice in their head. If you look at Brene Brown's YouTube video (Brene Brown: The Power of Vulnerability http://www.ted.com Uploaded January 3rd 2011) about "excruciating vulnerability" you come to the understanding that vulnerability is in fact the seat, the heart of innovation.

Kirsten: *I like that notion. It's an acknowledgement that teaching and learning are always at play. To say, "I don't know yet, I need to know more," is an opening.*

Don: Yeah it's really interesting. It's knowing that to be vulnerable is not a negative, it's not actually a criticism, it's okay. I'm going to digress for a second. There are students who sit in assembly and have conversations with students who aren't performing, I'll guarantee you, they are the people who never get up and perform. They don't know what it's like. This is connected to positive psychology. The student gets up and performs or they're in a band, or they're a soloist, a drummer, it's dance, it's music, whatever … there are some students who think, everyone in the audience wants me to fail. They're thinking, they're willing that. When in fact that's not what's happening. 99.9% of people are willing you to be successful, but the positive inner talk isn't happening for that student.

Applying that vulnerability concept, recognising and embracing it, knowing you can ninja that negative thought and turn it into a positive, that sort of thinking came out of reflecting as a staff on the question, "What do we need to do as teachers to develop positive thinking for ourselves and also for students?" This is really important, particularly in terms of advocating for kids. You can't walk down the corridor here… not that we have too many corridors, but you can't walk round the school and pretend you're okay, without someone knowing.

Whereas in a school where they don't have a focus on knowing students and advocating for them, you can pretend. There are students we would consider as A+ students who are a mess. The moment we invite them into a different kind of dialogue, something more personal, we might see a crack in their façade and actually wow, they were only just holding it together. I'm talking about kids who might have been in Thai – Burma border refugee camps, or whose parents immigrated some generations ago and whose home life is totally dysfunctional. Recognising that in every family, there's stuff that needs to be processed and understood, about who am I and what am I good at, what I need to be good at and how do I do that?

Kirsten: *Some kids might think that the main source of support is within the family, whereas you're actually opening up avenues of support enormously.*

Don: When we ask students to do pieces to camera at the end of the year, they say, "It's just like one big family here." In order to make those relationships happen, staff need to have a language. They need understanding. We don't ask them to be psychologists, we have a whole process of referral to outside experts, but it's about knowing the action research and inquiry we're doing into positive psychology is another layer to support mentors, to support teachers, to support the whole atmosphere in the school. Often students just need a scaffold. Say they think of their workload, assignment deadlines for the term and they think, it's too big, I don't know where to start. You need to teach them how it chunk it, show them, let's just start here. Decide what's the most important task. What's the most fun thing to do? What can you do quickly? Which teacher can you go to and say "Look please can you give me some help right now? I know I've mucked up but I really need to sort this out." Students just need to be given signposted pathways, scaffolds, to work forward.

We use action inquiry to extend skills for long term staff members, there's always something more for us to learn. There's a different way of doing something. For the graduate teachers, it's about sharing their knowledge with more experienced staff and vice versa. It comes back to collecting those arrows in the teachers' quivers, in terms of classroom management strategies, it's knowing which ones are really effective. For example, restorative justice is really strong in schools. That whole approach to repairing the harm when things go wrong, through dialogue, is all connected. Positive psychology inquiry is really just another element, to skill up teachers, and make sure they have sufficient awareness of themselves as educators and use language students can understand.

Kirsten: *So you're really refining skills for teachers, in asking them to collaboratively work out how they might then enact those refinements and be self critical and self aware...*

Don: ...and to bring it back to the wider school community. It's about consistency within the school, so that everybody is using the same language, has the same concepts going, even though there might be variation due to personality, relationships, things like that, but there is this mantra that works. You know there's a consistent rule, that when you walk inside the building your ear buds come out. I'm not going to have a conversation with you about why you have to take your ear buds out, I don't need to. So it's about making sure everyone is on song with that, it all works. It's about this collective communal responsibility...

Kirsten: *...which makes people feel safe doesn't it and therefore able to be vulnerable.*

Don: Yeah.

Kirsten: *And to learn...*

Don: You know it always amazes me and yet it doesn't at the same time, that we need processes for this kind of collective care. We need to articulate what we're doing, because teachers and students, they'll forget. It's a bit like, in times of crisis when a teacher's under pressure with a class, they'll teach in the worst imaginable ways that they themselves were subjected to as a student. It'll come down to, you know, flight or fight type stuff...

Kirsten: *...yeah, no one can think clearly when they're under extreme stress.*

Don: Yeah, so apply that knowledge to staff and apply it to kids, take the stress out where you can. I mean stress is good in moderation, it's just when it actually tips over it's a worry. Once again we get back to adolescence, you know it's body image, relationships, it's everything from a pregnancy scare for a girl, through to "no one likes me" as a boy, or "I'm isolated" or, "I think I'm same sex attracted." As teachers we deal with so many things, all at the same time. That is simply what it is. That's what it is to be in the job. Your job is not to just teach science.

So action inquiry is about experiencing and applying the theory, the understanding, the idea, and seeing how it works and then asking yourself in that reflection phase, so why did it work or why didn't it work or how can we make it work better? It doesn't mean the concept was wrong or bad, it might be the way it's been applied. We need to talk about our teaching and learning experiences in an exploratory way.

Kirsten: *Yes, when I do this, what happens? When I try this with x, this happens but when I do it with y, how is that different?*

Don: Yeah, you have two year 8 classes, you run this brilliant unit, it works with one class, doesn't work with the other, and that's because you haven't recognised who's in your class and what do they really need and what's going on for them.

One of the things we ask of our staff is to look at what are you teaching, and ask: "Why are you teaching it, and why are you teaching it now, and how do you know it works, and where are you going next?" Ask students to answer those same questions: "What are you learning?" "Why are you learning it?" "Why are you learning it now?" "How do you know you've learnt it?" "What does this learning connect to?" Because you need to know the connection between what you knew last month, what you're learning now and what you'll need to learn next month.

Kirsten: *And is that formalised, that kind of questioning?*

Don: Oh yeah absolutely...

Kirsten: *So it's about responsibility, having a language to talk about teacher and student learning, to talk about the complexity of education in meaningful ways, which is what I think you do really well here.*

Kirsten: *So it's making all the complex of dimensions of learning explicit.*

Don: Yeah. Hopkins and Craig talked about learning intentions being explicit, "Why am I doing what I'm doing today?"

Kirsten: *It's a question we all need to ask ourselves isn't it?*

Don: Yeah, the other one is, asking, "How am I being assessed?" before I start the task. Now I've been banging on about that since 1984. Students need to know how the work is going to be assessed before they start the task, so they've got some idea. I didn't know I had to put a red border around it and write my name on the top right hand corner. I remember being told off in primary school for that. Well you didn't tell me.

Kirsten: *Yeah that's right, it's about not knowing. You've been very generous with your time Don, so is there anything finally that you think needs to be out there about advocacy or mentoring, from the perspective of a school leader?*

Don: I think it has to come from the top. There has to be a sense of value in the process that's genuine. I think this is central to creating an environment in which students are encouraged to produce their best work. I don't think advocacy is easy. It requires a commitment and an understanding from all staff. Good teachers have always known that it's about a relationship with kids that is appropriate, that has boundaries. You need to be friendly, but not their friend in the sense that they might want it.

Beginning teachers will invariably make the mistake of being too close to the kids. So professional boundaries need to be in place. But at the same time you need to be able to say to the student, "I see who you are..." I'm trying to remember the African greeting: *I see you... and I see you too.* It's kind of like, that's what we do, see one another. Because I see you, I need to do something for you, because I can see you need help or I need to tell you you're doing a wonderful job.

It's kind of like advocacy can be so simple too. The parent who is so used to the school ringing up and saying, "Little Billy has been a pain in the bum again today and he just threw scissors across the room." Parents dread those phone calls, but when you ring up and say, "I'm just ringing to tell you that Billy's been fantastic today, that is absolute gold." It gets back to the kid and the kid goes "Oh, oh okay, well that teacher is alright then". Advocacy is really just about relationships and if you don't know that this kid in your class played in a grand final last night, why don't you know?

So it's a whole commitment to trust and collaboration. You can't do advocacy for 15 minutes a day. I'll emphasize that it's got to be a commitment. It makes a difference then, and kids know when you're not being genuine.

Kirsten: *They do. Young people are particularly discriminating I think, because they're open and they're working very much from that level of the here and now ...*

Don: I think also the teachers don't understand... some do, but often they don't understand how powerful they are, how much they can influence students. Sometimes there are gems in your life, when an ex student comes up and says, "I want to thank you," and you hear their stories.

Kirsten: *I look forward to coming back to hear more of your stories. Thanks so much Don.*

Kirsten Hutchison
Faculty of Arts and Education
Deakin University

Don Collins
Coburg High School

STACIA BEAZLEY

8. ELECTRONIC SUPPORT FOR ADVOCACY

This chapter documents the role of electronic questionnaires in assisting advocates and mentors in their work with students. A collaboration between a research team from La Trobe University and a group of Victorian schools saw the development of a set of online tools – the Student Achievement Inventory (renamed the Student Advocacy Instrument) which allow students to develop a profile of their interests, skills and attitudes, examine the ways they interact with their school, sort out their goals and plan for the future. Schools are able to get a picture of their student populations: how they learn, their attitudes to different subjects and the ways they are taught, students' ambitions and the obstacles they face in making the most of their schooling. Students are supported in reflecting on their learning and are scaffolded to develop greater understanding of their individual purposes and aspirations for learning. This chapter describes the potential contribution this instrument offers to school information systems, advocates, mentors and students.

INTRODUCTION

The SAI (Student Advocacy Instrument, formerly known as the Student Achievement Inventory) was developed as one component of a body of research known as The Advocacy Project. This tool was used within an Advocacy Program where, ideally, regular one-to-one meetings between students and teacher/advocates could take place. The purpose was to assist students to manage their learning and wellbeing through a trusting relationship where they feel both heard and understood. While schools were advised of this one-to-one structure as being optimal, some schools were limited in time and resources available to the program and therefore made adjustments to how they used the SAI within their school.

Why an electronic tool? The traditional role of a teacher has predominantly been to engage with students in a classroom setting where the main purpose is to 'teach' students. There are many definitions of the word 'teach', most of them focusing on the transmission of knowledge from a more knowing person to a less knowing.

However the purpose of the Advocacy Project was to invite teachers to take on the additional role of 'advocates.' In the introduction to this volume the editors argue that:

> Advocacy differs in some respects from mentoring as it is generally understood. The label 'advocate' has been adopted from the beginning, rather than 'advisor' or 'mentor', to emphasize a particular aspect of the relationship. The task of the

K. Hutchison & T. McCann (Eds.), Somebody Knows, Somebody Cares, 97–110.

teacher-advocate is not to manage the student's behaviour but to listen to the student and be a reliable support. This involves having an understanding of the student's background and motivation and being prepared to persevere with the relationship. An advocate is committed to making sure that the young person's point of view is heard if they are in conflict with a teacher or the school.

Hence the SAI online tool was created primarily to provide teachers with tools they could utilize in this new role of advocate. These tools took the form of student questionnaires, with responses used to generate meaningful conversation between advocate and student. An equally important role of these questionnaires was to support students in talking about personal learning topics that they may not usually discuss with their teachers. The premise was that students would find it more comfortable initially, to answer computer generated questions, as a prelude to discussing their answers with their advocates, to avoid beginning with a direct conversation which they might experience as an interrogation. An instrument with the capacity to store student data had the potential to become a useful research tool for teachers and schools. Over time, longitudinal tracking of themes and trends amongst groups of students could support whole school planning, decision making and cultural change.

SAI

User Levels

The SAI was developed as is an online tool accessible via a secure log in and password where users were assigned one of 4 access levels: Student, Advocate, Advocate Administrator and Principal. A 5th user level of Global Administrator also exists for the overall SAI Program Managers. The diagram below shows the functionality of each level.

The Core Tools

The SAI gives teachers and students practical tools that guide them into conversations and that can open up a new form of dialogue that supports kids to learn and teachers to teach in a mutually beneficial, and even enjoyable, environment. It gives schools accumulative data on student's attitudes to subjects, teachers, learning styles and school culture to name a few. This supports a process of more informed decision making for the school around changes that impact the whole school community. The 7 core tools within the SAI indicated in Figure 8.1. SAI access and function levels are accessible to all user levels and their purposes and functionality are described as follows:

1. Student Profile

Information gathered in the Student Profile provides the foundation for an initial discussion between a Student and their Advocate. It asks questions around the students' family life, cultural background, language spoken and how their physical

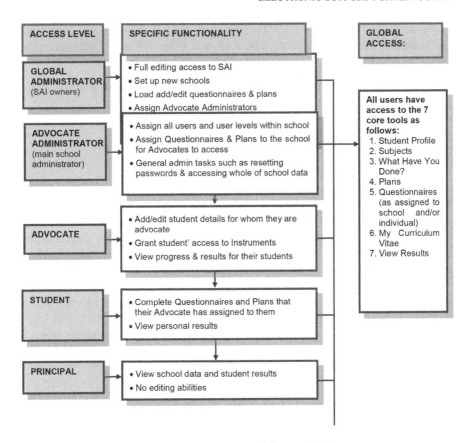

Figure 8.1. SAI access and function levels

environment is set up at home to support their schooling. Discussing this information helps students and advocates to understand how the students' home and personal lives impact their ability to be present at school and with themselves; information about after school work commitments, home computer access, suitable study space and family support. This important information provides insight into to the physical, emotional and psychological states students bring with them to school, and acts as a platform from which the most appropriate support can be given. It is important to review this information throughout the year, making updates as the students' situation changes.

Disengagement between students and their adult counterparts at school may have formed over a period of years and obviously requires time and solid commitment to change from both students and teachers, in order to bridge this gap. Having meaningful trusting conversations is the key step towards the possibility of any form of reconnection. The SAI provides a structural framework that can support these conversations to have meaning AND to show, over time, the progression, impact and outcomes that this type of relating can ultimately induce. Teachers' reports on the use of the SAI frequently referred to the value of the Profile instruments:

> I had no idea what was going on in Simon's life when he was at home. No wonder he is distracted in class.

> At the beginning of the year, I actually wouldn't know if our kids lived with their Dad or their Mum, or shared a room with 5 siblings. Now I do.

2. Subjects

The Subjects Instrument is a list of subjects and corresponding teachers that the student is engaging with during the year. Some of the other instruments cannot be used without this information, therefore students complete this section at the beginning of each year and update throughout the year as subjects and/or teachers change. For example, the Questionnaire titled *Teachers Classroom Management – Individual Teacher* asks the student to select which subject they are completing the questionnaire about. This supports the Advocate in knowing which teachers their students are having problems with. At a whole school, year or class level, administrators can generate reports showing themes in student responses towards particular teachers, which can be used to inform teacher performance plans and decision making around future professional development for teachers.

3. What Have You Done?

Many students have difficulty in identifying their skills that may be useful when looking for employment. The *What Have You Done?* instrument is an inventory of skills where students are asked to note what experience they have had in the categories of Paid Work, Unpaid Work & Work Experience, Family & School Responsibilities, Sports and Other activities. Each section asks for this information in relation to the Employability Skills Framework of the Victorian Education Department. This information links to the *My Curriculum Vitae* Tool which transfers information entered here and groups it under the employability skills headings in their CV, to provide evidence to back students' claims to possess certain skills. Each section is also pre-programmed with 2-3 examples of activities relevant to the topic to prompt students to think about their skills in ways they may not have previously. This tool has proven to be useful in providing students with a different perspectives on themselves and identifying their skills in social, community and employment settings.

4. Plans

The SAI hosts 3 plans for educational and career planning as well as a simple short term goal setting tool. The plans consist of:

- *career action plan:* a series of short reflective questions around subject choices and future course planning;
- *educational pathways plan:* more detailed plan inviting reflection on topics such as 'What I want to achieve', 'What I expect to learn this year', 'Extra activities' and 'How I will organise my learning;'
- *vocational pathways plan:* invites reflection on topics such as 'Favourite Subjects', 'Preferred Career Choices' and looks at Competencies & Strengths in relation to answers from the What Have You Done?

The plans are designed to assist students in reflecting on the purposes of their schooling and how they can make the best use of their time at school. As many students find it hard to feel motivated about their schooling, these tools help to put into perspective how schooling choices can support transitions into fulfilling and healthy life pathways into further study and employment.

5. Questionnaires

The Questionnaires are the main feature of the SAI and provide valuable information to support conversations between students and their advocates on a wide range of topics. There are a total of 28 questionnaires, within 6 categories: *About Me, About Me in My Classroom, About My Learning, About My Literacy, About My School,* and *About My Numeracy.* (Listed and briefly described in the Appendix to this chapter.) These questionnaires provide students and their advocates with immediate interpretive feedback, which can inform learning discussions.

For example, The Student Preference Questionnaire asks questions about how students like to learn and what they find boring. The responses are analysed and organized under categories which label preferred learning styles and produce a graph that gives the advocate and student a visual image of the students' personal style and how this impacts and/or supports their learning. Its focus is on 13 different dimensions such as Auditory, Kinaesthetic, Intuitive, Opening etc., as indicated in Figure 8.2.

Feedback for students not only indicates which approaches to learning students prefer – as indicated by high scores on the dimensions – but also tells students how they can benefit from developing other approaches which scored lower. The aim is not to categorise students as 'extraverted' or 'visual' learners, but to develop their understanding that there are many ways to learn and that limiting themselves to one particular way reduces their opportunity to learn. Having a better understanding of student learning styles and teachers' teaching styles & preferences allow for the possibility of changing the shared language between teachers & students to clearer forms of communicate both within and outside the classroom.

Schools choose which questionnaires they use, ideally determined through discussions between school Advocacy teams and the SAI managers, to develop a program that supports the schools' desired outcomes. The SAI provides teachers and

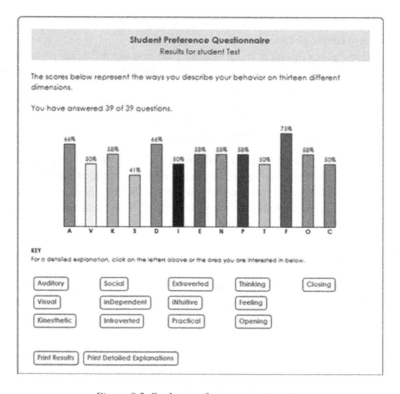

Figure 8.2. Student preference questionnaire

students with practical tools to guide conversations and potentially create new forms of dialogue that support student and teacher learning within mutually beneficial, and even enjoyable environments. It also allows schools to accumulate data on student's attitudes to subjects, teachers, learning styles and school culture, which can support more informed decision making to benefit the whole school community.

6. My Curriculum Vitae

The CV instrument asks students to complete general contact information, work experience, qualifications and references. Together with information imported from the *What Have You Done* instrument and the *Interests and Skills* Questionnaire, a CV is populated that is exported into a Word document for further editing and updating. This tool is valuable in showing students how schooling choices and external activities link to the possibility of gaining employment in the community.

7. View Results

The View Results section gives students and advocates an inventory of completed questionnaires and the ability to navigate directly to the results. Depending on the nature of the questionnaire, results are shown in question and answer style, or may be graphically represented. Students are provided with information on how they can use these results to better understand themselves as learners, identifying their strengths, weaknesses and offering suggestions for improvement.

FINAL COMMENTS

For students to grow physically, emotionally & spiritually, to have a sense of belonging within their schools and wider communities, they need to be free to learn. Together with learning about things 'out there,' they also need to learn about themselves, and to do this they must have space to reflect, to explore themselves and to feel understood, accepted and loved. They need to know that somebody is on their side, batting for their team and helping them to slide in to home base in their own way. These are the conversations, the conditions that parents are encouraged to create with and for their children. We must be aware that a substantial part of children's lives are also spent at school, with adults, teachers and others, who may be unaccustomed to being with their students or with themselves, in the way that Advocacy calls them to.

The SAI has been developed to assist students to understand themselves and to assist advocates to understand them. It does this by providing the stimulus for conversations intended to help students to make their experience of schooling engaging and purposeful. Some students have no trouble in talking about themselves, their problems and their dreams. Many teachers have the skills and confidence to initiate such conversations. For the others, students and teachers who are much more reticent and tentative about such things, the SAI can prove an invaluable resource.

Stacia Beazley
Executive Director
Advocacy in Education Research Group

APPENDIX

Questionnaire	Description	Results
About Me		
Good and Bad Things about Misbehaviour & Getting along Better in Class	This questionnaire is broken into three sections: 1) Why misbehaving is good 2) Why misbehaving is bad & 3) What students feel they may or may not be prepared to do to stay out of trouble in class.	Results are displayed for each of the three sections and displayed according to the scale of the answers given. Additional information appears at the bottom of the results page – viewable only for Advocates and not students – this information can support discussion around the students' misbehaviour from the perspective of Attention, Power, Revenge & Withdrawal.
How I Cope with Problems	This questionnaire looks at how students cope with things that worry them by asking a series of questions from the position of "When something bothers me, I......"	Along with listing all question responses grouped in answer sets the results also graph the answers based on the percentage of which the student Deals with, Shares or Avoids their concerns.
Interests and Skills	This is a general questionnaire that invites students to share about their personal interests and skills around topics such as music, games and sport.	Results are verbatim – question & answer style providing information to feed a discussion between student and advocate.
Reasons for getting into trouble in class	This questionnaire looks at the reasons a student may get into trouble in class by asking a series of questions from the position of "I get into trouble because......"	Results are presented via statements around the students' behaviour towards their Physical Environment, Learning, Wellbeing, Passivity, the Student-Teacher interaction and their Teacher's Student relationship.
Responsibility	This questionnaire looks at students' sense of responsibility towards teachers, students and members of their community. It also looks at whether students support others to behave responsibly.	Results are displayed via a graph and short statements in relation to responsibility of Self, Others and Community.

Questionnaire	Description	Results
Wellbeing	This questionnaire asks students to reflect on how they experience their school and family life.	The results provide a summary of the answers presented via short statements on General Wellbeing and Connectedness to Teachers, Friends and Learning.
About Me		
What helps me cope with concerns	This questionnaire looks at three different ways of coping and whether students find these helpful. These questions replicate those in the questionnaire 'How I Cope with Problems' looking specifically at *how helpful* the three coping styles are.	Along with listing all question responses grouped in answer sets the results also graph the answers based on how helpful it is for the students to Deal with, Share or Avoid their concerns.
When I don't come to school	This questionnaire asks students direct questions about their reasons for not coming to school.	Results are verbatim – question & answer style providing information to feed discussion.
About Me in my Classroom		
Good Teachers' Classroom Management	This questionnaire allows students to show which classroom management techniques they prefer. This can also assist teachers to reflect on their teaching styles to better meet student needs.	Results are graphed in six segments being; Punishment, Recognition, Discussion, Aggression, Hints & Classroom involvement. A short statement is provided that speaks to the student's preferences for each classroom management style.
Reactions to Discipline	This questionnaire measures how students react to teachers' classroom discipline techniques. This may assist teachers to reflect on how their disciplinary techniques impact students and hence their ability to learn.	Results are graphed in three segments: Fear, Justification & Disruption. A short statement is provided that speaks to the student's response for each segment.
Subject Related Attitudes	This questionnaire looks at student's attitudes to their most and least preferred subjects. They are asked to comment on the subjects themselves, their teachers and their levels of misbehaviour in these classes.	Results are graphed based on Misbehaviour, Teacher Popularity & Attitude towards the student most and least preferred subjects. [Note: the format of this results page is currently being developed]

(Continued)

105

Questionnaire	Description	Results
Teachers' Classroom Management – General	This questionnaire asks students to share their experience of their teacher's classroom management techniques. This questionnaire differs from 'Good Teachers' Classroom Management' as it asks of their *real classroom experience* rather than what they would prefer.	Results are graphed in six segments being; Punishment, Recognition, Discussion, Aggression, Hints & Classroom involvement. A short statement is provided that speaks to the student's experience of each classroom management style.
About Me in my Classroom		
Teachers' Classroom Management – Individual teachers	This questionnaire asks students to share their experience of their teacher's classroom management techniques *for a particular subject*.	Results are graphed in nine segments being; Punishment, Recognition, Discussion, Aggression, Hints & Classroom involvement as well as Teacher Emphasises Rules, Rights & Responsibilities and Communal Responsibility.
When I get sent out of class	This questionnaire asks students to share about their experience of being sent out of class. This may assist schools to assess teachers' rationale for throwing a student out of class and the impact this has on themselves, students and the class.	Results for this questionnaire presented in a report using short statements of the student's experience of being sent out of class.
About My Learning		
About My Schoolwork	This questionnaire will be useful for students to reflect on their view of themselves as a learner, their ability to set goals and long term plans, their ability to reflect on their own progress and to take others into consideration when they are planning their learning. Each scenario has a real and ideal setting.	Results for this survey are displayed in a graph based on four elements of meta-cognition: Personal *Narrative* Ability, *Intentionality* – ability to set goals and long term plans, *Reflection* – ability to self-reflect and make healthy judgements about personal progress, *Individuation* – ability to take responsibility for own work and consider others.

Questionnaire	Description	Results
Good Learning Skills	This questionnaire is subject based. The student first chooses the subject that they will be reflecting on and are then guided through a series of questions that look at seven important learning skills being: Seeking Assistance, Checking Your Own Progress, Planning, Thinking Ahead, Reflecting, Linking & Finding Evidence.	Results for each subject are displayed in graph form for each of the seven Learning Skills along with a summary of the skills the student is good at and those that require practice. Clicking on each of the Learning Skills will give a suggestion of how these skills may be practiced and improved.
Homework Survey	The homework survey helps students understand their relationship to their homework and what helps and hinders their ability to complete their homework.	Results are shown verbatim; question and answer in order to support dialogue and conversation.
About My Learning		
Responsibility for Learning: How much is given	This questionnaire explores how often students get the chance to decide what they will learn in class and how they will go about learning it. This questionnaire is useful for students to get a broader understanding of how they can be more in charge of how they learn.	Results are displayed in graph form under the four categories of Controlling Learning, Monitoring Own Progress, Leadership & Co-operative Learning. These results can then feed discussions around what students need to enable them to take more responsibility for their learning in areas that score low.
Responsibility for Learning: How successful	This questionnaire explores how well a student thinks they do when they get the chance to be in charge of their learning. This questionnaire can be useful to assist students in how they can become a better learner.	Results are displayed in graph form under the four categories of Controlling Learning, Monitoring Own Progress, Leadership & Co-operative Learning. These results can then feed discussions around how students deal with having more responsibility for their learning.

(Continued)

Questionnaire	Description	Results
Student Preference Questionnaire	These questions help students to identify their 'personal learning style'. In doing so students can begin to see how their preferences impact how they learn from the perspective of what they find difficult and what they find easy in a learning environment.	The results are shown in graph form and rate thirteen different learning styles being: Auditory, Visual, Kinaesthetic, Social, Independent, Introverted, Extroverted, Intuitive, Practical, Thinking, Feeling, Opening, Closing. Each style contains a link providing further information on the meaning of the style and what it may mean for students to have a low or high score in this area.
Technology Student Belief Scale	This questionnaire asks the student to reflect on their beliefs around their technology skill levels. This questionnaire is useful for discovering student ICT competency levels from beginners to advance users of technology.	Results of this questionnaire are graphed according to student's beliefs around their Beginning level skills, their Advanced level skills and specifically their Internet skills.
What I think about my subjects	This questionnaire asks students to reflect on which subjects they are feeling inspired and/or challenged by and why.	Results are displayed in question and answer style as answered by the student and can facilitate discussions around identifying strengths as well as support that may be needed to move through subjects identified as challenging.
About My Literacy		
Reading & Writing Survey	These questions are designed to help students to reflect on the types of reading and writing that they enjoy and/ or find difficult. They may see that they have strengths in some areas of reading and writing but want to improve in other areas.	Answers are verbatim; question and answer statements to generate conversation.

Questionnaire	Description	Results
About My School		
School Culture Questionnaire – My Actual School	This questionnaire and the one below (My Ideal School) both look at particular patterns of behaviour, attitudes and values that may be dominant in school culture. This particular questionnaire asks students to answer questions about *the actual experience of school* as it is right now.	Results for this questionnaire are graphed based on sixteen dimensions. Greek gods are used to represent each dimension archetypally, each having their own attitudes and behaviours. Pop-up windows are provided for further deals of each dimension.
School Culture Questionnaire – My Ideal School	This questionnaire and the one below (My Ideal School) both look at particular patterns of behaviour, attitudes and values that may be dominant in school culture. This particular questionnaire asks students to answer questions about *how their school would have to be* to satisfy their needs.	Results for this questionnaire are graphed based on sixteen dimensions. Greek gods are used to represent each dimension archetypally, each having their own attitudes and behaviours. Pop-up windows are provided for further deals of each dimension.
About my Numeracy		
10 Space (Geometry) Questions	This questionnaire asks students to respond to numerical questions based on their understanding of geometric space.	Results show the students' actual answer providing further information about how the question may be approached if it was incorrect.
20 Number Questions	These questions ask students to respond to a series of numerical equations and true/false questions to get a sense of understand and relate to numbers and numerical equations.	Results show the students' actual answer providing further information about how the question may be approached if it was incorrect.

(Continued)

Questionnaire	Description	Results
About my Numeracy		
Mathematics Questionnaire	The Mathematics Questionnaire asks a series of questions that allow the students to reflect on their understanding of what Maths is, how they feel about it and how important it is to them.	Results are verbatim – question & answer style in order to generate discussion around student attitudes to Maths.

KIRSTEN HUTCHISON AND BERNIE NEVILLE

9. THE HEART OF ADVOCACY

Implications for Schooling

In this chapter we synthesise the sets of knowledge and understandings about teaching and learning developed through the school-based advocacy programs described in this collection. Within a competitive educational climate of outcome – driven performance assessment, the centrality of emotional and interpersonal relationships in good teaching and learning is too often ignored. We endorse the value of the suite of 'caring attributes' evident in advocacy and mentoring programs conducted in professional educational settings, particularly in contexts where students are disconnected from education.

We know that disengagement and youth unemployment are more prevalent in areas of concentrated social and economic disadvantage. In Victoria, where the research described in this collection was conducted, youth unemployment (aged 15–24 years old) has reached 14.6% (Australian Bureau of Statistics, 2014) the highest yearly average for 15 years. We know that high youth unemployment is a disturbing dimension of social and political economies across the globe. Students who disengage from school prior to completion of secondary schooling, either through 'dropping out' or because they have been 'excluded' for behavioural reasons, are the group of adolescents least happy with their lives (Hillman & McMillan, 2005). The negative consequences of this are well known and include: long-term unemployment, social isolation, depression and anxiety, substance abuse and self-harming behaviours, or associated anti-social behaviours such as violence, vandalism, and criminal activities.

Young people not engaged in full-time study or work are twice as likely to be victims of crime, have fewer social resources to draw on, participate in fewer social activities, are less geographically mobile, are likely to have limited internet access and report significantly lower levels of satisfaction with their lives (Saulwick & Muller, 2007). While educational achievement continues to increase overall for young people, the Year 12 completion rates for the groups of young people whose stories are told in these pages, are of concern. Year 12 or equivalent completion rates are lower for Indigenous young people, for those living in regional, rural or remote locations, for young people from non-nuclear families or with parents who are not university educated (Stanwick et al., 2014). For these students located in regional or rural areas, the negative effects of disengagement or exclusion from school are

K. Hutchison & T. McCann (Eds.), Somebody Knows, Somebody Cares, 111–115.
© *2015 Sense Publishers. All rights reserved.*

amplified, by limited local employment or further study opportunities and lack of support services for young people experiencing isolation or mental health problems.

Students who disengage from school typically have experienced multiple traumas: poverty, homelessness, physical, mental and sexual abuse, drug and alcohol abuse, encounters with the juvenile justice system, mental illness, perhaps their own, or that of a relative. Inevitably, their lives are chaotic and their capacities to manage conflict, face challenges, deal with authority, trust others, learn, imagine alternative futures, are severely compromised. Their resources for mobilising the opportunities available through schooling are too often consumed by the effort required to survive. By contrast, their more fortunate peers, who complete Year 12, have a qualification that widens their capacities to make choices about their futures, making it more likely that they will lead healthy, productive & fulfilling lives. Completing school provides young people with a broader range of options for their economic future, promotes social inclusion, and provides greater protection against some of the negative consequences of unemployment and isolation, such as depression, substance abuse, or other self-harming behaviours, or engagement in anti-social activities such as violence or crime.

The Advocacy model of student support was developed within this context. The initial Advocacy Project (1998–2003), described in the chapters by Bernie Neville, Tricia McCann and Brendan Schmidt, was funded by the Victorian Department of Education. The Advocacy Project trialled two central components: the first, the establishment of a one-to-one relationship between students and teacher/advocates, who undertook specific responsibilities with regard to that student, who in turn, also accepted responsibility for their own progress. This relationship was informed by the second aspect of this innovative approach to student advocacy: online questionnaires relating to students' interests, learning preferences, goals, attitudes to school and literacy, numeracy and study skills. The Student Achievement Inventory, later renamed the Student Advocacy Instrument (SAI) was designed to increase students' self-knowledge about their learning, by identifying their strengths and weaknesses within a supportive environment. The digital environment of the SAI acted both as a tool for increasing reflexivity and metacognition about learning and also as a non-threatening environment for initiating conversations with advocates. Advocates helped students to act on the insights gained from the various questionnaires to address obstacles to learning, modify unproductive behaviours and develop self-esteem and confidence. Together, these two components were found to enhance school engagement for the students involved, as McCann, Schmidt and Beazley's accounts confirm. The self-assessment tools enabled advocates to individualise teaching and learning approaches, monitor student progress and share relevant information with other staff.

As the writers contributing to this volume have established, advocacy in schools is grounded in mutual respect, trust, teacher and student reflexivity and the cultivation of student agency. The key idea is the realisation that positive relationships between teachers and students engender engagement in schooling. The principles of advocacy and student mentoring are adaptable to fit the needs of a range of schools, undertaking the challenges of engage students in creative, meaningful learning. Whole school Advocacy programs have the potential to generate significant changes in school climates, in terms of teacher and student roles and relationships. While there is no formula for implementing meaningful Advocacy programs in schools, the intention to create conditions which scaffold positive teacher – student relationships is at the heart of this work, as the chapters by Hutchison, McCann, Walta and Collins illustrate. Equally however, as Walta and Hutchison have indicated, the establishment and sustainability of positive teacher – student relationships in contexts of concentrated social and economic disadvantage is fraught with challenges. As a holistic, multi-faceted approach to engaging and reengaging students in schooling, advocacy is not simply a 'strategy' but rather a complex and multi-layered set of understandings and stances underpinning teachers' work in schools. Designing and implementing programs appropriate for individual school contexts requires deep understanding of teaching and learning within communities, understanding of engagement and dis-engagement from schooling, understanding of adult and adolescent psychology, understanding of educational leadership, understanding of resistance to change and of course, time.

It is widely accepted that teaching is one of the most stressful occupations (Johnson et al., 2005). Teachers participate in numerous emotionally intense interactions with students every day and have a large number of emotional demands placed on them in comparison with other professionals (Brotheridge & Grandy, 2002). These emotional demands inevitably impact on teachers' health and wellbeing, potentially contributing to emotional and physical exhaustion, leading in extreme situations to 'burnout,' and cynicism about teaching, to decreased job satisfaction and sense of personal worth (Guglielmi & Tatrow, 1998; Shan, 1998; Vendenberghe & Huberman, 1999). These emotional demands are likely to be intensified in schools with significant proportions of students experiencing the compounding effects of multiple disadvantage, who are more likely than their more privileged peers to disengage from learning. One of the key dimensions of advocacy work in schools is the provision of professional learning for teachers on how to listen without judgement to students. Advocacy professional learning draws teachers' attention to their own counter productive tendencies, such as reactivity, in order to scaffold students' reflection on their own learning and foster the growth of more efficient habits. This requires teachers to draw on their own emotional repertoires and develop skills in regulating their own emotions (Brackett et al., 2010), in order to provide a safe haven for students in conflict with themselves and with others in their immediate school environment. Emotional intelligence is "the capacity to regulate one's own and others' emotional states" (Brackett et al., 2010: 407). Teachers involved in the research described in this volume were aware that their capacities to control and manage their own emotions contributed to their efficacy as teachers, to their classroom management skills and to their capacity to foster engagement in learning, derived from productive, trusting relationships with their students. In the process of modelling emotional regulation and discussing emotional intelligence with their students, teacher advocates also experienced increased professional satisfaction and more sustainable careers as educators, a finding supported by British research (Brackett & Caruso, 2007).

Advocacy then, contributes to teachers' capacities to articulate and manage and regulate their own emotions and those of their students. The professional learning in interpersonal skills informing their work as advocates allows teachers to model emotional intelligence to the students they are advocating for. This results in reduced incidence of conflict, healthier interpersonal relationships with students, and calmer and more productive learning environments. Thus, the Advocacy approach to student support is a powerful mechanism to enhance emotional wellbeing and learning in secondary schools. It requires commitment on the part of teacher/advocates, which extends beyond regular contact, counselling and assistance in developing learning plans and study skills. Teacher/advocates commit to never giving up on a student, to advocate for the student in any dispute with the school, ensuring that the student feels supported, acknowledged and respected. Perhaps most importantly, Advocacy holds potential to reshape teacher-student relationships and teaching and learning practices. For the schools involved in the Advocacy work described in this volume, many of the participating teachers expanded their awareness of students' perspectives on various aspects of their schooling experience and in the process, strengthened teacher-student relationships. Teachers developed their capacity to listen and support students, which in turn led to the evolution of increasingly sophisticated, differentiated teaching and more effective classroom management skills. The provision of sustained systems of one-to-one-support for students, including the digital student self-assessment tools lea to improved rates of school attendance and retention, and a reduction in removals from class for the participating students.

If Advocacy proves sufficiently flexible to fit the needs of a range of schools, and effective in engaging students in learning, it has the potential to reshape the hostile school climates experienced by a significant proportion of middle years and senior secondary students at risk of disengaging from schooling. Targetted development and implementation of advocacy programs, designed for the unique realities of individual school communities, hold the potential to reshape teachers' work and student engagement with schooling, into meaningful, compassionate, dialogic teaching and learning: the heart of advocacy.

REFERENCES

Brackett, M. A., & Caruso, D. R. (2007). *Emotional literacy for educators.* Carey, NC: SEL Media.
Brackett, M. A., Palomera, R., Mojsa-Kaja, J., Reyes, M. R., & Salovey, P. (2010). Emotion-regulation ability, burnout, and job satisfaction among British secondary school teachers. *Psychology in the Schools, 47*(4), 406–417.
Brotheridge, C. M., & Grandy, A. A. (2002). Emotional labour and burn-out: Comparing two perspectives of "people work". *Journal of Vocational Behaviour, 60,* 17–39.
Guglielmi, R. S., & Tatrow, K. (1998). Occupational stress, burnout and health in teachers: A methodological and theoretical analysis. *Review of Educational Research, 68,* 61–69.

Henry, J., Barty, K., & Tregenza, K. (2003). *Connecting through the middle years: Final evaluation report*. Melbourne, Australia: Department of Education and Training.

Hillman, K., & McMillan, J. (2005). *Life satisfaction of young Australians: Relationships between education, training and employment and general and career satisfaction*. Melbourne, Australia: ACER.

Johnson, S., Cooper, C. L., Cartright, S., Donald, I., Taylor P., & Millet, C. (2005). The experience of work-related stress across occupations. *Journal of Managerial Psychology, 20*, 179–187.

Ocean, J. (2000). *Advocacy evaluation* (Unpublished). Melbourne,Australia.

Saulwick, I., & Muller, D. (2006). *Fearless and flexible: Views of gen Y. A qualitative study of people aged 16 to 24 in Australia*. Melbourne, Australia: Dussledorp Foundation.

Shan, M. H. (1998). Professional commitment and satisfaction among teachers in urban middle schools. *The Journal of Educational Research, 92*, 67–73.

Stanwick, J., Lu, T., Rittie, T., & Circelli, M. (2014). *How young people are faring in the transition from school to work, foundation for young Australians*. NVCER.

Vendenberghe, R., & Huberman, A. M. (1999). *Understanding and preventing teacher burnout: A sourcebook of international research and practice*. Cambridge, UK: Cambridge University Press.

Kirsten Hutchison
Faculty of Arts and Education
Deakin University

Bernie Neville
Adjunct Professor
Faculty of Education
La Trobe University
Co-Ordinator, Bachelor of Holistic Counselling
Phoenix Institute of Australia